Please remember that this is a library book,
and that it belongs only temporarily to each
person who uses it. Be considerate. Do
not write in this, or any, library book.

To Joyce

EDUCATION
AND
HUMAN
VALUES

JOHN MARTIN RICH
UNIVERSITY OF KENTUCKY

ADDISON-WESLEY PUBLISHING COMPANY
Reading, Massachusetts
Menlo Park, California • London • Don Mills, Ontario

This book is in the

ADDISON-WESLEY SERIES IN EDUCATION
Social, Behavioral, and Philosophical Foundations

Consulting Editor
Byron G. Massialas

FOREWORD

This series is designed primarily for those who will assume leadership roles in the schools of today—the teachers. In a rapidly changing world, schools are required to develop new educational roles and perspectives; more than ever before they pay attention, directly or indirectly, to the social, political, and economic conditions of the larger society. In this new era, education is considered to be an investment in national development, and equalitarian principles increasingly provide the basis for educational policies. Such factors as the socioeconomic status of children, their ethnicity, regional differences, occupational aspirations, and their beliefs and values have been gaining in importance. These and similar factors determine to a large extent the educational environment needed to generate in children a motivation to learn, to think critically, and to develop defensible ideas about themselves and society.

Consciously or unconsciously, teachers impart norms of the individual's role in society. Regardless of their subject of instruction, teachers have, for example, the potential for performing a political socialization function—they are in a position to convey to children knowledge about and attitudes toward the political system. Children begin, at a very young age, to internalize the political norms which characterize the system; e.g., participation, social trust, political efficacy, etc.

It is our firm belief that an effective teacher should become thoroughly familiar both with the substantive content of certain of these topics and issues and with the role of the school in dealing effectively with emerging social problems. In turn, the teacher's role is not only to introduce these topics and issues in the context of civilization's past wisdom, but to motivate the student to seek new viewpoints and solutions through his own inquiry skills and creative talents. It is not presumptuous to reaffirm that mankind's future largely depends on the quantity and quality of education of our youth.

Specifically, the books in this series are designed to help the reader understand the following:

1. The functions of education as a social agency and its interrelations with other social agencies.

2. The historical roles of schools and changes in these roles mainly resulting from urbanization and industrialization.

3. The role of education both as an institution and as a process, as it affects personality formation, socialization, cognitive development, and the self-concept of the individual.

4. The impact of education on the social, economic, political, and intellectual development of a nation.
5. The influence of education on human values—their formation, justification, adjudication.

In connection with the above, the series attempts to indicate how knowledge-claims in the field have evolved and what particular skills and procedures of social research have been used. The focus is on selected unifying concepts, e.g., socialization, culture diffusion, elite formation, human values, and economic and political modernization as they relate to education. Each volume singles out an aspect of the relation between education and society and deals with it in depth. Each author, while looking at his topic from the perspective of a scholarly discipline, be it history, political science, sociology, or philosophy, tries to draw from other related fields as well.

We hope that these volumes will offer educators and teachers new insights into our understanding of education and the emerging world culture and will open new doors for additional work and study in the social, behavioral, and philosophical foundations of education.

Byron G. Massialas

PREFACE

It has been frequently observed that we are living in an age in which vast technological changes have wrought widespread transformations in social and cultural conditions. The dislocations following in the wake of such changes have eroded some cherished values of the past and brought about conflicts and uncertainties in others. The effects of all this have generated feelings of apprehension and instability. Some have sought a sense of security by immersion in the group in an attempt to regain their identity; others have rushed headlong toward any doctrine or ideology that offered certitude and a panacea for the afflictions besetting the human condition.

This state of confusion has not left education unscathed, for all too frequently the uncertainties and conflicts in the larger society are reflected in its educational institutions. The pace has quickened in the search for new ways to bring about improvements in educational conditions. Considerable energy is currently being expended in the study and implementation of a multiplicity of devices and programs by educational technologists; unfortunately, educational values have not received the same degree of attention. Since all areas of education are undergirded by values, and since the most basic decisions that must be made with regard to the future direction of education are value decisions, we neglect them at our own peril.

It is hoped that this work will mark a fruitful beginning for the student of education and human values. It provides an examination and an analysis of some of the value issues found in education today and proposes alternate solutions to these problems. The student should note, however, that the book probably raises more questions than it answers. On a number of issues there are no clear-cut answers, of course, and in other cases an attempt has been made to raise and delineate issues and to stimulate the student's thinking so that he will be challenged to engage in further inquiry. The book is organized around cultural, organizational, moral, and aesthetic values.

The author gratefully acknowledges the assistance of a number of persons. Professors Byron G. Massialas of the University of Michigan, A. Stafford Clayton of Indiana University, and Ayers Bagley of the University of Minnesota read the manuscript in its entirety and offered many helpful criticisms and suggestions, which resulted in a number of improvements in the manuscript. I should not wish to overlook my colleagues in the Division of Foundations of Education at the University of Kentucky, who have been a continual source of stimulation. I also wish to thank Mrs. Lois Mitchell for her careful and efficient typing, and my parents for their encouragement. Of course, none of these persons is responsible for any shortcomings that the book may have; I assume full responsibility for any deficiencies.

J. M. R.

Lexington, Kentucky
March, 1968

CONTENTS

CHAPTER ONE

CULTURAL VALUES
AND EDUCATION

Introduction

If a visitor from another planet, who possessed no knowledge of American society in general should visit our schools, he would probably be able, after sufficient study of our educational system, to tell us a great deal about the society at large. He might find, for instance, that democratic principles of education (including respect for the dignity and worth of each individual) are widely espoused by educators but infrequently observed in practice. He would be correct in inferring that the ideals of democratic life are habitually extolled in theory but often not honored in practice.

Schools in all cultures tend to reflect the cultural traits and patterns of society. Traditionally, education has served as the conservator of the heritage; occasionally—and more frequently in recent years—educators have urged the schools to take a leadership position and play a central role in the tasks of social reconstruction. To what extent they are capable of fulfilling this latter role and, moreover, whether it would even be desirable for them to do so, are questions that we will want to examine in greater detail in this chapter.

But in the long history of empires and civilizations, education has seldom served as a reconstructive force; instead, it has been an instrument for preserving the dominant cultural values of society. Educational institutions invariably have been controlled by the group or class holding the reins of power, and they have used the schools to advance their own interests. In addition, throughout the ages educators have failed, for a multitude of reasons, to stress universal education as a prime objective. In civilization after civilization, education has unabashedly served an elite. It has perpetuated, reinforced, and strengthened the values of a select group, usually to the detriment of the majority. And the denial of educational opportunities has been used (although not in all cases successfully) to further protect the position of those in power. This is a characteristic feature of educational systems, not only in the past but even today in many countries throughout the world. It may be observed that in England the "public" schools are operated largely for the benefit of the upper classes; the Communist party in Russia, the Roman Catholic church in Ireland, and the Caucasian middle class in the United States has organized the school system to the disadvantage of other groups.

However, it is well known by students of educational history that America was the leader in providing universal, free public education. Some claim that this is undoubtedly one of America's great democratic achievements. Some have held that "our schools have kept us free." Henry Steele Commager maintains that in the historical struggles that shaped our country the schools provided an enlightened electorate, helped weld national unity, assimilated millions of immigrants by teaching them the cultural patterns and expectations of their new country, and served to break down artificial social and economic distinctions through a common educational system.* Assuming that we accept Commager's criteria of freedom, there is certainly evidence available to show that the schools have performed such tasks.

However, we may note with Boyer that universal education is also found today in the Soviet Union, and thus, may not be exclusively characteristic of democracies; on the other hand, the fostering of an understanding of society, the promotion of intelligent criticism, and the defense of institutions necessary for unrestricted criticism

---

* Henry Steele Commager, "Our Schools Have Kept Us Free," *Life*, October 16, 1950, pp. 46–47.

are not characteristics of totalitarian systems.* These are essential features of democracies, he contends. If we accept the belief that the schools should promote these functions, there is some evidence to show that the schools have not kept us free.† The promotion of orthodoxy, the silencing of opposition, the censorship of educational materials, the intimidation of educators by special interest groups, and innumerable violations of academic freedom highlight the history of American education. Once again, any answer that could be given to the question "Have our schools kept us free?" would depend largely on one's criteria of "freedom" in a democracy. We will not attempt to examine the multiplicity of interpretations of the concept of freedom that have been advanced and debated in the past.‡ It also seems that Commager's argument raises the complex question of causality in history; that is, to what extent can we claim that the schools brought about the conditions in American culture that Commager cites? §

We would be remiss, however, if we failed to make certain points at this time. First of all, the process of schooling can do a commendable job of socializing the young and making them "obedient" citizens. It can do this by teaching students to act unquestioningly on the basis of what they have been taught and by reinforcing prescribed behavior through the use of a system of rewards and punishments. Obedience, docility, and orderly performance of routine duties become the hallmarks of the system.

We are not advocating that schools should stop providing social training or that authority should be abolished because of such abuses. The problem is one of establishing authority without tyr-

---

* William H. Boyer, "Have Our Schools Kept Us Free?" *The School Review*, **71** (Summer, 1963), pp. 222–228.

† The most important studies illustrating this thesis are those by Howard K. Beale, *Are American Teachers Free?* (New York: Scribner's, 1936), and *A History of Freedom in American Schools* (New York: Scribner's, 1941).

‡ For a more thorough exploration consult George H. Sabine, *A History of Political Theory* (3rd ed.; New York: Holt, Rinehart and Winston, 1961).

§ This is a problem in the logic of historical inquiry that can be pursued in depth in Ernest Nagel's *The Structure of Science* (New York: Harcourt, Brace and World, 1961), Chap. 15.

anny and combining discipline with humanity. It is exceedingly unfortunate that such a creative combination is seldom found. Authority becomes tyranny whenever it treats human beings as things to be manipulated rather than persons to be nurtured and respected.

If the citizens in a democracy are to be effective, they must have, at the very least, opportunities to question, weigh arguments, and arrive at decisions on the basis of reflective examination of competing alternatives. Also, an individual cannot fully realize his abilities as a person without the opportunity to develop his intelligence by pursuing ideas wherever they may lead. Censorship and restrictions on inquiry are anathema to the citizen's development and his effective participation in a democratic society. As John Stuart Mill noted in his *Essay on Liberty:* "*Since the general or prevailing opinion on any subject is rarely or never the whole truth, it is only by the collision of adverse opinion that the remainder of the truth has any chance of being supplied.*"

Suffice it to say, there is much about public education to justify pride; yet the record is badly marred at many points in our history by deliberate attacks and restrictions on freedom of inquiry. And we know that without freedom of inquiry education is really not possible. Certainly there is great room for improvement in the years ahead.

The Relation between Education and Culture

Actually, the relation of formal education to the larger culture may be any relation prescribed by those who hold the reins of power. The relation is not fixed and universal; it can be characterized by variety and susceptibility to the nuances of societal changes.

It has been thought that the nature of the child is a primary determiner of the relation between education and culture. Taking a cue from the progressive concept that education, to be effective, must recognize the developmental characteristics of children and youth and the modes of instruction appropriate at the respective stages of development, some have held that society cannot impose external demands upon schools that conflict with the factors of development and still realistically entertain the belief that education will be successful.

In the history of education some societies, in structuring their educational systems, have virtually ignored the characteristics of the learner as a prime guide in determining the relation of schooling to society. Those in power either have not been sufficiently enlightened or have not found it to their advantage to use these characteristics as criteria. Formal education follows more frequently than it leads: it follows the dictates of society, and society at times makes demands upon education that ignore what may be best for youth.

From anthropological studies we learn that human beings have great plasticity and adaptability; personality and behavioral patterns of an unusual variety can be cultivated, even though our ethnocentrism often leads us to believe that the personality patterns cultivated in our society are truly the "natural" and sensible ones, while those found in other societies are odd and foolish.

Even if we have schools that do not violate the nature of the learner and his developmental characteristics, however, we still have not accounted for the relation between school and society (beyond acknowledging the fact that society should make certain provisions for its educational institutions). It appears that the recognition by society of the learner's nature would provide, at best, a necessary condition and, at least, a negative condition that would proscribe in a limited area certain actions that society should not take in order to avoid infringing upon provisions for effective learning.

The same holds true if we examine teaching. We could study the teaching act from the point of view of speech acts, symbolic behavior, physical behavior, role playing, interaction analysis, or some other process. It might be possible through such studies to acquire a more complete knowledge of the teaching-learning process and the conditions that would improve the process. But the goals of education in a complex technological society cannot be derived from the study of the teaching act. Decisions about how to improve the process of learning can be made on the basis of these studies, but what is to be learned and the value of different types of knowledge and skills are not derived from such studies (any more than they would be from a study of the developmental characteristics of youth).

According to one point of view, the function of the school is to provide skilled manpower in order to meet existing demands and exigencies in society. This seems plausible when we recall that since the launching of Sputnik society has belatedly recognized a need for more scientists and engineers. It becomes the task of the school, then, to fulfill whatever needs arise at a particular time.

But one may demur at this latter statement on the grounds that education alone cannot overcome every deficiency in the larger society; other institutions and agencies have their roles to play, and with greater institutional cooperation and interchange of ideas, tasks confronting society can be brought under greater control and handled with greater effectiveness.

With the welter of demands placed on them by society, schools find themselves in the position of a sailboat on a stormy sea. Because of insufficient navigational planning and inadequate regard for weather conditions, the boat is tossed and turned by every gale. As a result of insufficient planning and the absence of a clearly formulated political philosophy attuned to the latest thinking in human affairs, society has been battered by unforeseen and unpredicted technological and political developments, and has been able to cope with them only by the establishment of *ad hoc* committees. In addition, the rapidity of change in Western societies in the latter half of the twentieth century has increased to overwhelming proportions the pressures on the schools to meet unforeseen demands. Thus the schools toss and turn from one demand of society to another. What is needed is sound planning on the part of the larger society. But one cannot plan intelligently without a clear sense of direction. Thus, without a clearly formulated social philosophy that will take a stand on the major issues of the day, long-range planning makes little sense, and we are left with *ad hoc* proposals to deal with social exigencies as they arise.

In recent years perceptive observers have noted that schools can no longer educate to prepare for existing occupations and present-day functions of society. Instead they must prepare people for a world that may be radically different from the one existing at the moment. On the basis of the few available long-range studies of our society, one can make probability statements concerning the types of skills and abilities that will be needed by our youth. Or the schools can provide a general education that will cultivate modes of reflective thinking that will enable tomorrow's adults to develop the requisite skills and abilities for living in a rapidly changing society.

The traditional interpretation of the role of schooling has been that schools initiate the young in the ways of the culture by serving as an agency of socialization. There has also been wide support for the view that revered values and traditions, too priceless to be subjected to the risk of loss, will be preserved by transmission from one generation to another.

Although this task is not easily performed, it appears to be clearcut and unequivocal. However, determining what is to be transmitted is a highly complicated process; selection is both quantitative and qualitative. First of all, there is such a vast cultural heritage that the schools are automatically restricted to transmitting only a small portion of it. Secondly, not all of the heritage is deemed desirable and worthy of transmission.

It is evident that the task of selection is critical. But before selection can be undertaken intelligently, one must clearly determine what values will guide the selection process. The content of the curriculum is not self-evident; the values that will underlie any curricular pattern must be made conscious, so that they can serve as working tools in the process of selection. And educators should study values more carefully than any other aspect of education if curricular programs are to rest on sound foundations.*

The process of selection is not the only critical concern of educators. After choices of content are made, there is still the problem of deciding how the teaching of such heritage will be of value to youth in a rapidly changing world. Since many social, economic, and technological developments in this century are unprecedented, the question arises as to how history and related studies can be a guide to the world of tomorrow. With the repudiation of the formal discipline theory, justifications for allotting large segments of time for subjects believed to be essential features of our cultural heritage and the mark of an educated man must come under increased scrutiny and appraisal. If our schools are not to be sequestered halls of learning, remote and unconcerned with the pressing problems of our civilization, future discussions of "teaching the cultural heritage" must realistically and straightforwardly confront the ways in which a study of our heritage can be brought into fruitful interchange with new knowledge in all disciplines.

---

* The use of educational standards for purposes of evaluation is discussed in Chapter Two.

Our educational institutions are expected not only to transmit the heritage but also to prepare youth for future occupations, develop sound character, promote physical health, and teach the ways of the culture. Thus we see that there is a reciprocal relationship between education and the culture. Up to this point we have looked primarily at cultural influences and demands on education, but we will also want to observe that educational institutions, in addition to their roles as cultural transmitters and socializers of individuals, have an impact on the larger culture by performing certain distinctive functions that are not principal functions of the larger society.

TWO FUNCTIONS OF EDUCATION

The School as Community

The first of the distinctive functions is that of the school as community. Leading nineteenth-century educators believed in general that the school served as a socializing force and taught the children of immigrants the ways of American culture. Even after the establishment during this century of immigration quotas, progressive educators thought of the school as a miniature community, a place where the learning experiences of youth were continuously related to life. Schools had earlier been thought of as remote places separated from the mainstream of the community. Children went to them reluctantly, submitting to the routine of assignments and recitations, which were sometimes meaningless or irrelevant to the concerns of children. The traditional school was characterized by some progressives as a place where the child learned by rote inert material unconnected with the larger community and life as a whole. The child gleefully welcomed the end of the school day, so that he could get on with the business of living.*

A vital characteristic attributed to the public school was that it had the potential to be the highest expression of American democracy;

---

* Whether these strictures against traditional forms of education are overdrawn, and whether the progressive movement met with any marked success can be studied further in Lawrence A. Cremin, *The Transformation of the School* (New York: Alfred A. Knopf, 1961).

since all the children of all the people would be represented, the school would be the only place in our culture where persons of divergent backgrounds would have the opportunity to interact and participate in processes of democratic learning over extended periods of time. Within the larger society, whether in business, industry, the professions, or politics, interaction of persons of divergent social and economic backgrounds, if it existed at all, was arbitrarily restricted or limited. But in the schools artificial barriers could be dissolved and equal opportunities to learn the process of democratic living could be provided. Actually, there were those who claimed that this was possible also in certain institutions or agencies in the larger society. That distinctions were clearly being made on the basis of race, color, nationality, religion, or economic station in life, however, was evident to all who observed actual practices rather than permitting themselves to be blinded by preachments. Certainly minorities who were discriminated against could readily cut through the Fourth of July oratory and ask for action to give such pronouncements credibility and currency. But those who have not experienced the suffocation of opportunity through discriminatory practices have never found it easy to develop a social conscience sufficiently sensitive to recognize cant and hypocrisy for what it is.

Educators hoped that the public school, attended by representatives from all social classes, races, religions, and nationalities, could provide opportunities for interaction and appreciation of differences that young people might never gain in the larger society. Furthermore, school experiences would carry over, and there was hope that as the young people took their places in society as adults, their democratic spirit would direct their efforts toward maintaining our institutions on democratic principles. It was in the public schools that prejudice and artificial distinctions acquired in the larger society could be eventually overcome through democratic participation. Although this sanguine hope of educators was not entirely unrealistic (for in a number of schools such democratic participation did take place as part of the distinctive function of public education in America), too often the deeply entrenched social attitudes and concomitant practices which precluded the realization of this ideal were either improperly diagnosed or, when diagnosed correctly, attacked with inappropriate strategy and insufficient resources.

Before examining the impediments to democratic participation in public education, we should note that even if the idealistic hopes of educators had been realized in this regard, the sources of power obstructing the attainment of democratic participation in the larger society would have to be reformed before one could realistically believe that youth would not be continuously frustrated in their attempts to live by the ideals learned in school. We should also observe that whenever the larger society fails to reinforce through its own practices the ideals and attitudes learned in the schools, the likelihood that youth will be able to make such learning a part of their conduct is greatly diminished. Social reforms are needed in all our institutions if the ideals of democracy are to become a reality in everyday practice.

There are several obstacles to the realization of these ideals in American public education. One of the fundamental problems has been the withdrawal of children from the public schools and their enrollment in private and parochial schools.*

Of the many church-sponsored schools that have been established, the Catholic parochial schools have the largest enrollment. Catholic schools carry forth religious education by infusing religion into all subjects in the curriculum.

The democratic ideal of community is limited then, first of all, by the existence of a school system other than the public one, a system in which a major religious group consciously controls the education of the youth of its faith. It should be recognized, however, that the people of a state cannot compel all children to attend public schools.†

An even more serious problem than the extent of democratic participation in the public schools is the financial support of public education itself. The attempt of Catholic schools to get funds by

---

* For a discussion of the historical development of this problem, see John S. Brubacker, *A History of the Problems of Education* (New York: McGraw-Hill, 1947), Chaps. 11 and 17.

† The compulsory public school attendance issue was decided by the United States Supreme Court in 1925 (*Pierce v. Society of Sisters*). But no question was raised concerning the power of the state reasonably "to regulate all schools, supervise and examine them, their teachers and their pupils." The state can require that "all children of proper age attend some school."

breaching the wall of separation between church and state traditionally inferred from the First Amendment leads to the estrangement of those who support the public school. Should such attempts prove successful, they could undermine the very concept of public education. After years of inadequate support, the financial foundations of public education would be gravely threatened. And with the success of one major religious group, other religions would probably follow suit and gain state support to establish their own religious schools. The demise of public education as we have known it would eventually follow, not only because its financial support would have been depleted, but also because its one-time supporters would have turned their allegiance to their own religious schools.

Returning to the concept of the school as community, we note that the continued growth of private secular schools, organized to provide education that will appeal to higher socio-economic classes, has meant that in some public school systems (particularly in those parts of the country where the private school concept is widely supported) the student body lacks adequate representation from the upper-middle and upper classes. In addition, parents of children who attend private schools are seldom avid supporters of the public schools. Since persons from these social classes are likely to wield an influence in their communities that is disproportionate to their numbers, the absence of their wholehearted support for public education is a serious loss indeed. Furthermore, wherever the public school lacks widespread support, it is unlikely that the ideal of children from all backgrounds learning together the ways of democratic living can ever be more than the ideal that it is.

The most serious denial of equality of educational opportunity in our history has been the deliberate establishment of segregated school systems, which has had the effect of branding Negro children as unequal and unworthy of attending white schools. With the historic desegregation decision in 1954 (*Brown v. Board of Education*) and with subsequent pronouncements by the United States Supreme Court in the following year, school districts were directed to proceed "with all deliberate speed" in desegregation of school districts. That the process has moved at the proverbial "snail's pace," in defiance of the Court and to the chagrin of supporters of civil liberties, has brought the federal government, through the Office of Education, to deny funds to those districts which fail to develop and carry through a desegregation plan within a stipulated period of time.

The deliberate discriminatory treatment of an entire race in certain sections of the country is not only a denial of the concept of community but also one of the most serious blights on American democracy in the annals of discrimination and mistreatment found so frequently in our history. As the Supreme Court has stated: *"To separate them from others of similar age and qualifications solely because of their race generates a feeling of inferiority as to their status in the community that may affect their hearts and minds in a way unlikely ever to be undone."* In addition, students of human nature have long held that the process of discrimination not only is damaging to the victim but also can hurt and eventually destroy the persecutor. Those who inveterately discriminate pay an awesome price to maintain their prejudices.

With increasing frequency in recent years the ideal of community has been progressively vitiated in the North by the exodus of the middle class to the suburbs. The need for urban renewal in some of our metropolitan areas today is staggering, and with insufficient financial support at all levels of government, the process of deterioration is likely to worsen in the immediate future unless prospects for massive expenditures and systematic, long-range planning suddenly improve. This does not appear likely at the moment. With federal expenditures for defense exceeding one-half of the national budget, and with the inability or unwillingness of municipalities and state governments to find and allocate sufficient funds to improve the cities, the centers of our metropolitan areas and their school systems are likely to deteriorate even further.

As groups of various minority races and nationalities increase in number in our cities, white middle-class Americans escape to the suburbs, not only to find better school systems for their children, but also to avoid living near members of minority groups to which they hold certain aversions. This has brought about de facto segregation and denied the concept of community. Thus many schools in northern communities are more homogeneous than ever before in matters of race, nationality, and social class.

The concept of community, at one time heralded by educators as nurturing democratic participation and fostering the highest ideals of our society, has been partially eclipsed by the parochial and secular private school movements, by conscious and deliberate discrimination on the basis of race, by the neighborhood school, and by restricted housing covenants and the patterns of homogeneity that ensue. Although the concept of community is at least partially realized in some school systems, the factors that militate against its attainment are serious indeed; and although they have been made less damaging in some areas through programs of social change, they have become more firmly entrenched in other areas.* The concept of community will not become an actuality in most American schools until citizens as well as local leaders become sufficiently informed on the issues and attain a point in their development at which they genuinely desire such reforms and deliberately work toward their realization.

Education as Social Criticism

In traditional educational arrangements, the teacher was an authority figure and the student's role was to follow the teacher's dictates and demands. The teacher, at least in some traditional schools of the past, was looked upon (or expected to be looked upon) as a fount of knowledge pouring information into the craniums of students who would then obediently give it back on tests.

To some the above description may seem a caricature, but others may find that it resembles their own public schools today. In any case, with the rise of modern science, and later with the introduction of experimental modes of thought into instructional programs, many schools began using reflective modes of inquiry rather than primarily appealing to authority and authority figures. If a democratic way of life is to become more than merely a sentimental idealization of lofty goals, it must transform the way in which people relate to their fellows. And since democracy depends on its citizens to make wise and intelligent choices, the schools have a critical role to play: they must see that individuals have the knowledge and skills necessary to make such decisions.

---

* One approach—not a model of community itself but moving toward it—is a proposal to have learning pursued in three contexts: school; laboratory-studio-work; and community seminar. See Fred W. Newmann and Donald W. Oliver, "Education and Community," Harvard Educational Review, 37 (Winter, 1967), pp. 61–106.

Democratic societies are founded on the belief that an educated citizenry can govern itself intelligently and make wise decisions. Citizens can develop their ability to choose intelligently not only by learning from the writings of others, but also by participating in a program that affords opportunities to make careful observations, formulate hypotheses, test ideas in experience, and engage in critical discourse on issues of moment. As youth discover and test the meanings of ideas within experience and learn to use the method of experimental inquiry in their search for knowledge, they acquire the understanding that knowledge is developed and verified through the human mind and imagination. And whenever this way of approaching life becomes a characteristic part of one's thinking, then appeal to authority, tradition, folklore, or transcendental truths breaks down, and ideas are accepted only after they have been tested in experience. The student learns that no matter how exalted the idea or tradition, if it is put to the test of experiment and fails to produce the conditions or consequences that it predicts, it is not valid. Thus, the experimental mind *"is the mature mind in the sense that it can operate on the basis of probability; it retains its confidence in the worth of intelligence in a world that makes knowledge a human necessity, and yet denies absolute finality to any particular human conclusion."* *

Most institutions of society endeavor to see that their members perform certain rituals and acts and carry out behavior patterns in accordance with prescribed social roles; they usually discourage any criticisms of the rationale underlying these processes, and they rarely are receptive to searching criticisms of the institution itself. But since education is designed not only to transmit heritage and to socialize youth, but also to promote reflective modes of inquiry that critically examine society and its institutions, including the school itself, such a process becomes a distinctive function of education in a democratic society, since it is unlikely to be nurtured and encouraged in any institution other than the school. As Belth puts the matter:

Few, if any, institutions "educate" their members to question the grounds of their own existence in such a way as to produce funda-

---

* From *Education and Morals* by John L. Childs, p. 166. Copyright, 1950, by Appleton-Century-Crofts, Inc. Reprinted by permission of Appleton-Century-Crofts, Division of Meredith Publishing Company.

mental changes in institutional direction, meaning, and function. Few urge their members to continue free investigation, at no matter what point, in order to come to conclusions which might contradict institutional goals and concepts. And no institution other than the school is dedicated to nurturing the very means of criticism of itself and of all other institutions.*

Yet, unfortunately for the health of both education and society, "nurturing the very means of criticism of itself and of all other institutions" has not been seriously fostered in education because there is widespread opposition in many quarters of society to such a practice, and also because in many cases teachers lack the requisite competencies to put such ideals into effect. The closest that American society has come to the accomplishment of these ideals has been in our most prestigious universities where academic freedom has enjoyed a long history of strong support. The public schools, on the other hand, have been subjected since their founding to innumerable infringements and restrictions on academic freedom and the freedom of students to inquire.† Although freedom of inquiry and the right to make critical assessments of society and its institutions have been more severely limited in some periods than in others, the public school has suffered restrictions throughout its history.

Some citizens may believe that to permit schools to encourage freedom of inquiry either will bring about disrespect toward society and its cherished traditions or will in some manner undermine democracy. However, one may wonder whether genuine respect is fostered by an uncritical acceptance of a society and its institutions, and whether the best way to cultivate respect is by presenting only the strong points of our way of life while glossing over its shortcomings and failure to measure up to professed ideals. As for the contention that critical assessment of our society would undermine democracy, so much the worse for democracy if it is so defective that it cannot withstand the probings of young inquiring minds. So long as young people understand the methods of reflective and experimental inquiry and use it correctly in defining

---

* Marc Belth, *Education As a Discipline* (Boston: Allyn and Bacon, 1965), p. 49.

† See Beale, *A History of Freedom in American Schools.*

problems, formulating hypotheses, gathering, interpreting, and testing evidence to confirm or refute initial hypotheses, citizens should not fear that youth will undermine a way of life for which adults claim a superiority beyond question. The claim is inconsistent, for those who make it fail to consider how they arrived at their conclusion. Certainly it should be possible to subject the reasoning and evidence by which such a conclusion was reached to careful scrutiny, in order to corroborate or refute it. If this way of life is superior, why should those who support it fear that its foundations will collapse when thoroughly examined? And how can those who deny students the right to inquire into such matters claim that they are acting consistently and in accordance with the democratic principles they espouse?

The anti-inquiry forces have an additional objection. Public school students are too young and immature to question the foundations of our institutions. Their impressionable and immature minds may cause them to be easily swayed and indoctrinated by ideologies inimical to democracy. Perhaps when they attain maturity and have a stake in their communities, we are told, they may be in a position to undertake such an investigation. At exactly what age level this state is likely to be attained is unclear, however. Presumably, the student will not reach it before he is in college, perhaps not even until he is at the more advanced level in college. Thus young adulthood would probably be a more appropriate time to undertake such a study.

However, one may legitimately wonder whether a person who has been inculcated with the values of a certain way of life, who for many years has been told about its incontrovertible virtues, and who has been exhorted, either overtly or tacitly, never to question them will in adulthood find it possible to reverse the process and focus his dormant powers of reflective inquiry on society. Certainly his ability to inquire will be woefully underdeveloped and will not suddenly blossom forth because some authority has opened the gates to its use. If youth truly are to develop the ability to inquire, they must use it throughout their educational careers. There seems to be no good reason why the teaching of reflective inquiry cannot be systematically included throughout the years of a student's formal education in ways that are consonant with his abilities and with the degree of his overall maturity at each level of his development.

The root of the problem lies in the fear and misconceptions of the citizens themselves. Societies usually get the quality of education they deserve, and so long as misconceptions of democratic education prevail in certain communities and sections of the country, it is probable that restrictions on freedom of inquiry will persist— if not increase in magnitude. A society that is open, flexible, and self-renewing is always vigilant with regard to the educational effects of its social institutions upon its individual members. Such a society adopts as a normative procedure the continuous appraisal of its institutions in terms of this criterion. Not only the schools, but all the institutions of society begin performing a truly educative function. At that time, citizens can continuously engage in learning the ways of democracy, for the role of each institution is to reflect and illuminate—not only to indoctrinate and inculcate— the values of the larger society. Under such circumstances, learning becomes an ongoing lifetime function, and knowledge of the democratic process and its meaning and import for human relations are more widely shared, understood, and practiced.

DIMENSIONS OF THE CULTURAL CRISIS

The twentieth century arrived in an atmosphere of hope and promise, of general confidence that relationships among peoples everywhere would be increasingly humanized and improved. This noble hope was soon to be shattered. By mid-century man could look back on two world wars, the political isolation of societies, totalitarian revolutions and the concomitant dehumanization of relations among peoples, and poverty and squalor juxtaposed with opulence and waste. No wonder the minds of many men turned from an optimism engendered by trust in the inevitability of progress to apprehension, doubt, and distrust. *"Some find refuge in a fanatical faith and in reliance upon infallible leaders of the people; others seek evasion of responsibility in simplifying and comforting panaceas; many are simply wary and have given up the attempt to understand and to act."* * Many false prophets arose, meanwhile, ready to present a multitude of solutions. But these did not eradi-

---

* Hans Kohn, *Political Ideologies of the Twentieth Century* (New York: Harper and Row, Torchbook, 1966), preface.

cate the cause of the disorder and, in consequence, anxieties worsened when false panaceas were exposed. There appeared and persists an ominous realization that the *"grounds of our civilization, of our certitude, are breaking up under our feet, and familiar ideas and institutions vanish as we reach for them like shadows in the falling dusk."* *

The optimism generated during the Enlightenment—the belief that civilization is steadily progressing toward a higher level of refinement and perfection—pervaded a frontier spirit in America that sought to tame the wilderness through industry and ingenuity. The proclamations of nineteenth-century educators, with their hopes and aspirations for the common school in its role of democratizing the culture, reflect a similar optimism. But this spirit was not always shared by the literary figures and utopian thinkers of the day.† From Marx to Nietzsche and from Thoreau to Dostoyevsky there are forebodings of a new age fraught with social and political upheavals and undermined by the erosion of the traditional values of religion and morality. Such omens seem to have arisen from a plethora of interpretations and perspectives which had as common denominator a challenge to folk wisdom.

We have entered today an age of highly technological, developed societies, a period that, according to Boulding, could be referred to as a "post-civilized society." ‡ In many ways, too, we have entered an "accidental century" (to borrow Harrington's descriptive term),§ a century in which the West has revolutionized its social structure, economy, and technology, but without revolutionists, without long-range planning. This "revolution" has caught countless people unaware and unprepared for the type of world in which they live;

---

* Arthur M. Schlesinger, Jr., *The Vital Center* (Boston: Houghton Mifflin, 1949), p. 1.

† For a juxtaposition of the darker perceptions of life held by some Americans and the optimistic views of professional educators, see Maxine Greene, *The Public School and the Private Vision* (New York: Random House, 1965).

‡ Kenneth E. Boulding, *The Meaning of the Twentieth Century* (New York: Harper and Row, 1964).

§ Michael Harrington, *The Accidental Century* (Baltimore: Penguin Books, 1966).

many are incapable of comprehending, much less controlling, the forces that shape their lives.

Both world wars were fought to overcome advancing oppression and to restore peace in the world. Neither war, however, brought a reasonable balance of power or lasting peace. Although a few hardy optimists imagined that the end of the Second World War represented an end to our troubles, developments on the world scene soon revealed that this was a false hope. Niebuhr has suggested that instead of discovering peace we discovered that we are living in an era between two ages.

It is an era when "one age is dead and the other is powerless to be born." The age of absolute national sovereignty is over; but the age of international order under political instruments, powerful enough to regulate the relations of nations and compose their competing desires, is not yet born. The age of "free enterprise" when the new vitalities of a technical civilization were expected to regulate themselves, is also over. But an age in which justice is to be achieved, and yet freedom maintained, by a wise regulation of the complex economic interdependence of modern man is powerless to be born.*

Steps have been taken to bring about a workable system of international law, but there has been much less progress than the protagonists of a world community had hoped. We have endeavored to achieve a balance of power, following policies of the past; yet every participant ultimately will seek to improve his own position while regarding similar efforts of others as attempts to disturb the balance.

The world is no longer made up of many large powers that in some mythical way can create a balance of political force on the international scene. There are fewer large powers today and many smaller powers with diversified interests and cultural backgrounds. Those who hope to establish a regulated international community must recognize that the issues involve the entire field of international life where power is exercised; it is not possible, in any sense of the word, to solve the issues, except by drawing the smaller

---

* Reinhold Niebuhr, *Discerning the Signs of the Times* (New York: Scribner's, 1946), pp. 39–40.

nations into political deliberations and policy formation. Yet, even though the smaller powers would gain a voice in these deliberations, clearly some centers of authority must be established if international order is to have direction. In view of the enormous cultural and ethnic diversity in the world, it appears at this time that only the preponderant power of the great nations can provide an adequate core of authority for a minimal world order. For a considerable time to come, then, the international community will have few elements of inner cohesion and will not be able to benefit from a common base of culture or tradition. However, the fear of international anarchy among the great powers, although not as powerful as the fear of a common and concrete foe, may act as a stabilizing force and give the nations time to create an international community.

The task of the school in this matter is not unequivocal. Some hold that the threats to our sovereignty can partly be offset by inculcating the ideals of our nation and imbuing patriotic fervor in the minds and hearts of each generation.

Others, however, would have the schools teach and extol the values that would accrue from an international community. According to this viewpoint, we live in a time of crisis, a period in which the basic values of our culture are in a state of widespread confusion and disorder; with the imminent threat of nuclear annihilation, our best hope lies in teaching the need for a world community.

A third contingent supports the view that teachers and students should be free to explore reflectively the human condition and the conflicts and cleavages in our culture. All areas of our culture should be carefully examined and subjected to the critical test of experimentation. The teaching-learning process should be the result of combined efforts: students should be free to arrive independently at defensible positions, and teachers should see that students acquire the tools and abilities of experimental inquiry they need for making intelligent decisions.

Each of these positions has some merit; but each in its own way, if relied on exclusively, would restrict one's vision. Certainly, an appreciation of the ideals of our nation and the promotion of patriotic feelings have merit so long as such teachings are not imparted with the express intent of blinding students to the shortcomings of our culture and its need for improvement.

Then too, the need for an international world order, which offers the hope of bringing peace and stability to our troubled times, should never be dismissed lightly (even though obstacles in the way of its achievement are numerous and obdurate). However, to teach the need for world order without making a fair and impartial examination of alternative proposals is to derail the educational process and to shortchange students. In addition, it might develop habits of thinking that would lead to intolerance of other positions.

Nonetheless, in reflective examination of all major alternatives, one should not regard all proposals as being of equal merit if some have previously been tested and found wanting. The concept of national sovereignty, for example, because it has proved inadequate and even aggravative in international relations, cannot stand on equal ground with proposals that aspire to go beyond the deficiencies of the sovereignty concept. Of course, such proposals must also be evaluated on their own merit. One should not be deluded into believing, however, that because all positions are examined, the school is scrupulously guarding a position of neutrality. The process of constructing a curriculum and selecting its content involves earlier value decisions on educational aims and selection criteria. In addition, the use of the method of experimental inquiry represents a value decision, a choice which its proponents support by comparing its outcomes with the results of alternative methods of instruction.

Cultural Changes and Education

There have been widespread changes in the American family during the past century. Especially significant is the shift from an extended family organization to that of the nuclear family. Formerly size of family was not a liability, especially in rural life, and economic, religious, and educational functions were performed under family dominion. Today, however, the large family constitutes a financial burden, and furthermore, the basic economic, religious, educational, and recreational functions have been assumed, for the most part, by other institutions and agencies. With the need for greater specialization in vocations and with the relinquishment of numerous social functions once assumed by the family, schools have been expected to play a larger role in the total development of youth.

Youth may find themselves beset by increasing pressures to postpone their entrance into the competitive job market. To encourage this, they may be paid to remain in school or to work on government-supported projects. They may very well experience increasing alienation as jobs become scarce. Their emotional turmoil is not likely to be mitigated by the gap between the generations as members of the younger generation find that they are better educated and more closely attuned to a changing world than are their parents.

Cybernetics will pressure youth to choose their occupations on the basis of talent rather than subjective preference. Not only the unskilled, but also many white-collar workers and managers will find their jobs eliminated by automation. The need to be retrained several times in a working lifetime is already with us on a limited scale, and this characteristic of modern life will become more important except for those in the professions. The professional will find his services more in demand, his work week more lengthy, and the demands of his specialty will require a lifetime of effort devoted to the acquisition and use of new knowledge.

Some members of the older generation may find themselves stripped of lifetime jobs, alienated from the ideas and beliefs of the younger generation, and disillusioned because their treasured values and ways of living have been eroded by rapid social changes. The gap between new knowledge and the ability of the population to understand and envision its significance for society is likely to widen critically unless provisions are made for our institutions and agencies, as well as the communications industry, to begin serving, in a systematic and coordinated manner, a truly educative function.

A paramount danger to our society, as the older meaning of work is transformed by automation, is the hiatus between the highly educated few who decide what decisions the machines will make and the consuming masses on the other side. With the increasing inability of people to grasp the specialized knowledge on which decisions affecting their lives are based, the dialogue between the decision-makers and the masses breaks down. And we cannot appeal to our original values of work to find our way out of the impasse. *"So it is at that point in history at which the Western work ethic is finally in sight of subverting almost every remnant of tribalism, feudalism, and aristocracy on the globe, it ceases to be a practical guide for the culture that gave it birth."* *

In order that the gap between the decision-maker and the average citizen may not become unbridgeable, it will be necessary for all institutions to begin serving their respective educative functions; for all citizens to be imbued with the conviction to pursue their education throughout a lifetime; and for the mass media of communication to be safeguarded from the danger of control by several powerful groups, to be allowed the freedom to express a diversity of views on problems of democratic life, and to promote, in cooperation with institutions and agencies of society, the continuing education of citizens. None of these tasks will be easy to accomplish. Citizens will first need to recognize the urgency of promoting such practices, and they will have to continue to support them vigorously after they have been established. For democracy will have to be revitalized, reinterpreted, and promoted by each new generation; it is not an ideology that, having been promulgated by our founding fathers, needs no further examination or reconstruction. In order for democracy to maintain its strength and its viability, it will need to be interpreted anew in light of changing times and conditions, and its principles must enter the thinking of all citizens and play a central role in their lives.

Consensus in the Democratic Process

If we are to make democracy viable and functional during the latter half of the twentieth century, we may need a consensus arising out of a democratic social philosophy. However, we do not at present have a stable, integrated society agreeing on basic norms, and consequently the order and direction necessary in education no longer exist, and confusions resulting from the absence of widespread agreement on educational goals reflect the uncertainties and conflicts in the larger society. In this transitional period, a clear concept of educational authority and a consensus on the role and function of the school are missing. One may wonder, then, how a viable agreement on the goals and purposes of education can be secured.

---

* Harrington, *op. cit.*, p. 259. Reprinted with permission of The Macmillan Company. Copyright 1965.

It could be argued that the schools cannot ignore the confusion and conflict in society by constructing a sheltered educational environment that will shield youth from the value conflicts of our time. Neither can schools impose upon youth a way of life that would be unacceptable to society; for not only would the schools find such instruction contradicted by value patterns of authority in society—and thereby sacrifice their effectiveness—but they would also be exceeding their legal authority. Educators who undertake such a course of action without regard to public opinion or political forces in the community would, according to Stanley, *"quickly discover that the ultimate control of the school has not been vested in the teaching profession."* *

There are a variety of ways of gaining consensus. The characteristic technique in a totalitarian state is the use of force and coercion. Any social philosophy used to achieve a consensus in a democracy must be consistent with the fundamental tenets underlying democratic life. Thus an authoritative or absolutistic social philosophy is inconsistent with and inimical to democratic values. Any social philosophy that is viable for democratic life must be cogently and systematically developed so that it can bring some semblance of order and direction to the widespread value conflict in contemporary life. It must also provide a theory of social change by which the meaning of such change can be assessed and interpreted and by which criteria can be established for ascertaining whether the direction the change is taking is in keeping with democratic life. Moreover, such a philosophy must be sufficiently open to incorporate new knowledge from the social and behavioral sciences and sufficiently flexible to reconstruct any of its basic assumptions whenever they become obsolete. Such a philosophy must have a wide appeal if it is to be useful as a basis of consensus. Above all, it must be normative in the most important sense, by directing its central focus on human values and the conditions in society that promote growth and fully functioning persons.

However, such a social philosophy may not really be necessary. Perhaps what is needed instead is a clearer understanding of democracy and its workings in the lives of people. A social philos-

---

* William O. Stanley, *Education and Social Integration* (New York: Teachers College, Columbia University, 1953), p. 129.

ophy erected to bring about consensus on societal norms and to offer direction for education must at all times be consistent with democracy. Why, then, do we need to construct or appropriate a social philosophy when democracy itself, in many ways, is a social philosophy? The problem seems to be one of encouraging citizens to acquire a sufficient working understanding of democracy and to use it in their daily lives as a basis for human relations.

Another faction argues instead that a systematic reassessment of democratic principles is needed if their significance and application in a new cybernated age are to be better understood. The breaking up of old concepts of national sovereignty, for example, has caused a severe impact on other concepts such as patriotism and the national state; and new developments in world trade, such as the European Common Market, lead to a reappraisal of economic concepts previously considered most functional for a democracy. There are other issues—many of which have already been discussed—whose reassessment could lead to new interpretations and applications of outdated democratic principles.

Still others hold that what is needed is a better understanding of how to play the game of life in such a manner that the rights of all are protected. Persons in a democracy need to reach agreement on the general rules regulating their behavior; they need not agree on the particular ends toward which each aspires as an individual. Indeed, one of America's strengths is its encouragement of diversity. We live in a pluralistic culture in which persons of divergent beliefs, religions, nationalities, and races are accommodated, if not assimilated. Our great strength has been our success at encouraging this diversity and at the same time forging a unity out of it. This unity has always been imperfect (consider, for example, the coercive methods government uses during wartime to maintain it). Yet, despite the diversity, revolution has not been a feature of American life. Differences have been settled by negotiation and by legislation. The minority is always encouraged to hope that by accepting the principle of majority rule and then providing constructive criticism of the weaknesses of the majority position, supplemented by effective techniques of persuasion, it may some day become a majority.

Another difficulty with social philosophies that proclaim that they will lead the way out of the wilderness of value confusions and will provide far-reaching solutions to contemporary problems is that such visionary ideals tend to be unconnected with action in the present. Any social philosophy that disregards the means by which its proposed ends are to be achieved, and thus is unrelated to present-day conditions, is little more than a verbal proposal. Such a philosophy may even be dangerous for democratic-minded citizens to take seriously, because it can be invoked to sanction almost any practice.

To insist that an act becomes democratic in relation to its goal without consideration for the means employed for its attainment, is to be guilty of advocating that ends justify means. The democratic process is predicated on the search for human means for the attainment of human ends. Anything less is a violation of the basic tenets of democracy. As Lindeman has stated: *"The doctrine of maximum compatibility between means and ends is the source of democratic morality. It is the morality that needs to be taught and exemplified in education."* *

One can, on the one hand, perceive dangerous conflicting goals and forces in American life and, on the other hand, recognize that the observance of democratic procedures provides the necessary safeguards against the likelihood that such forces will bring about widespread disorder and anarchy. Although the historic function of American public education has been to weld unity out of enormous diversity, its task has also been to nurture healthy forms of diversity. Unity is gained through teaching the principles of democracy and encouraging individuals to incorporate those principles into their lives; unity is also fostered by promoting knowledge and appreciation of a common cultural heritage. Diversity is encouraged by teaching students respect for differences and by promoting tolerance and understanding of various ways of life. Students can also be shown that their lives may be immeasurably enriched by interaction and exchange of ideas with persons of divergent backgrounds.

One of the striking facts about American life in this century is the blurring of differences and the increasing homogeneity of tastes. With mass consumption of similar products, mass communication (which has a tendency to lessen differences), and the growing

---

* T. V. Smith and Eduard C. Lindeman, *The Democratic Way of Life* (New York: New American Library, 1951), p. 153.

other-directedness of the population, the pendulum seems to have swung toward homogeneity in recent decades. If we are to have a meaningful unity based on the exercise of democratic principles, the task of the schools at this time must be to protect cultural diversity.

The United States also appears to have moved from being a nation to being a national authority, with the different sectors of policy, economy, and culture more unified through this authority. That this is actually a consensus may be open to question, in view of the fact, mentioned previously, that the gap between the decision-maker and the layman has appreciably widened in recent years. In any case, however, the manifestations of this unity in actual practice resembles a consensus on matters of public policy.

American education has never had a central authority for the formulation of its goals and the direction of its programs. But with the increase in funds originating from the federal government and the growing interest and the large investments of private industry in educational technology and its employment in the curriculum of the nation's schools, a more centralized focus of educational authority is rapidly developing. Whether the combined policies and activities of government and private industry prove consistent and mutually reinforcing remains to be seen; however, all indications at this time point toward a growing centralized focus.

In conclusion, the only consensus that is both viable and necessary is agreement on the rules by which democratic principles become effective in society by being incorporated into the daily activities of individuals. Yet such a consensus, although providing a sense of unity through the observance of common principles, would not lead to uniform patterns of thought and action, since the cornerstone of democracy is unity through diversity, brought about by the promotion of respect for individual differences within the framework of democratic living.

EDUCATION AND THE HEALTHY SOCIETY

If a society is to grow and prosper—not only materially and technologically, but also in the creative potentials of its individual members—it will need to concern itself with the conditions that foster healthy growth and development. It has been said that the human organism is unusually plastic and malleable, since man has created and lived under, with varying degrees of success, an unusual variety of cultural patterns. There has been a tendency for those who do not accept a system of absolute truths that transcend cultural boundaries to take virtually the opposite view that the deleterious effects of absolutism and ethnocentrism can be negated by the attitude that one culture is just as good as another, that no one should impose his values and way of life upon another person. Perhaps when it first appeared, the subjectivist attitude served as a salutary corrective to the more inflexible and ethnocentric views of man. However, while rectifying some of the untoward consequences of the absolutist view, it left the door ajar for the free entry of a number of other excesses. The subjectivist view has not been able to show, by means of its primary assumptions, why the cultural patterns in Nazi Germany or Fascist Italy, for example, were pernicious to human development and unworthy of man.

The problem is to find some tenable position between, on the one hand, the rigidity, ethnocentrism, and uncompromising attitude of the absolutist and, on the other hand, the lack of common values and the tendency to uphold personal preferences as grounds for values of the subjective relativist.*

Absolutists apply the same yardstick to all situations irrespective of conditions, persons involved, or the particular culture. They judge all individuals, situations, and cultures by a set of absolute standards. Absolutism leads to insensitivity, inflexibility, provincialism, and arrogance.

In contrast to subjective relativism, absolutism does recognize an objective, nonhuman element. It avoids the problem, raised by the subjective relativist, of seeing each value relative only to the context in which it is found, which leads to the denial of common values; yet this factor is far too slight to outweigh the serious shortcomings of absolutism.

---

* The line of thinking at this point generally follows that developed in Houston Smith, *The Purposes of Higher Education* (New York: Harper and Brothers, 1955), Chap. 2; and David Bidney, "The Concept of Value in Modern Anthropology," *Anthropology Today*, ed. A. L. Kroeber (Chicago: University of Chicago Press, 1953), pp. 682–699.

What is needed is an attitude recognizing that individuals, situations, and cultures are not identical, while at the same time seeking grounds for values in their situational contexts that are more objective than personal preference.

First of all, we can speak of values that are good for a particular individual under certain conditions without basing our choice on personal preference. For example, a physician may prescribe a brace for a person who has a spinal injury, but one cannot generalize from this that all individuals should wear braces, or even that all who have spinal injuries should wear braces. Yet this decision, which applies to a single individual and is not generalizable, is based not on personal preference but on a medical diagnosis and a therapeutic procedure for correcting an injury. The prescription of a brace for the particular individual is a situational value choice that has its basis in an objective decision.

However, it should be observed that, although we have situations that are not generalizable but whose objectivity for the particular context can be established, most situations are generalizable. If this were not true, we would be unable to utilize previous experience and experiences accumulated in our culture as a basis for action; we would have to face each problem anew, without the aid of previously acquired knowledge and past experience. The fact that each situation has certain unique elements does not mean that it has no elements in common with others. Thus we have values that are good for a group of situations that have common elements. The existence of a few elements in the group that are not identical does not invalidate generalizations, since generalizations do not rule out exceptions. Whenever the elements of a group of situations are sufficiently similar, generalizations can be made. For example, the rule that one should drive on the right-hand side of the road holds as a generalizable principle except under emergency conditions.

We also believe that there are values, such as monogamy, which are valid for our own society, but may not be for others. Similarly, most of us (except those who take the absolutist position) recognize that there are values in other cultures which, although differing from our own, are nevertheless valid for them. Some cultural anthropologists condemn ethnocentrism and intolerance of ways of life differing from our own, while they seem ironically unaware of the extent to which they are treating uncritical tolerance and uniform appreciation of all cultures as absolutes. Their position denies that any valid statements about values can be made for all mankind and insists that values are evolved for a culture out of the particular historical experiences of that culture. Thus there can be no absolutes or fixed standards. There are, this position concludes, no universal values because there are no absolute values.*

The above position leaves us at a loss as to whether a particular culture or civilization in general is progressing. Are there certain basic human values that all cultures should promote in order for people everywhere to be able to live fruitful and meaningful lives and to have the opportunity to develop their abilities? Industrialized cultures need individuals who use their abilities in creative and imaginative ways. Yet each culture encourages some abilities and discourages others. Our culture, for example, confers greater prestige on the scientist than on the artist. Human abilities are not narrowly confined: they find expression in a vast range of activities. Every society imposes restrictions upon those activities that conflict with the larger goals and values of the culture. Societies differ greatly in their willingness to tolerate a wide range of activities by its members. We will want to explore certain characteristics of psychological health that should be encouraged by a society that wants its citizens to operate on a high level of productivity.

As an alternative to both absolutism and extreme cultural relativism or subjectivism, it has been proposed that there are certain universal criteria of psychological health irrespective of whether a culture, or a particular group in a culture, believes that its norms are the only "normal" ones.† We need to examine at this point some of the criteria of psychological health and the types of cultural conditions which promote it.

Psychological health is no longer characterized by the concept of "adjustment," at least not in humanistic psychology, the "third

---

* For a more thorough development of this position, see Ruth Benedict, *Patterns of Culture* (Boston: Houghton Mifflin, 1934); Melville Herskovits, *Man and His Works* (New York: Alfred A. Knopf, 1948).

† See A. H. Maslow, *Motivation and Personality* (New York: Harper and Brothers, 1954); Erich Fromm, *The Sane Society* (Greenwich, Conn.: Fawcett Publications, 1965).

force" in psychology (the other two are behaviorism and psychoanalysis). Adjustment indicates a conformity to conditions without the flexibility, openness, and creativity characteristic of a fully functioning person. Even more serious, one can be considered *adjusted* to society, so long as he complies with its norms, even if the society fosters intolerance, brutality, thought control, and denial of opportunity. One can be *adjusted* to a gang of thieves also, so long as he demonstrates that he is a good group member by complying with the gang's norms.

There are also tendencies in our world, more pronounced in the East than in the West, to view self-denial and the control and inhibition of impulses as the only desirable way to conduct one's life. Some religions hold that human desires are of the flesh, that the body is wicked and evil and therefore its wants should be ruthlessly suppressed if the spirit is someday to enter the kingdom of heaven. An alternative to this viewpoint is that an individual can lead a productive life only if certain basic needs are satisfied.*
Needs arrange themselves into a fairly definite hierarchy on the basis of their relative potency. Before an individual can actualize his full potential, certain needs in the hierarchy must be fulfilled. These begin with physiological needs and move to the needs of safety, of love, and finally of esteem.† According to this point of view a life of asceticism and denial of basic desires can never lead to the full development of the individual. In countries where there is widespread economic deprivation, and among groups in our society whose basic physical needs are not met, the individual finds it impossible to develop his whole potential. Thus many cultures throughout the world have condemned their members to something far less than complete development and the productive use of abilities.

---

* Maslow, *op. cit.*

† Concepts of "hierarchy" and "needs" are not without their difficulties. John Dewey criticizes a hierarchy of values in his *Democracy and Education* (New York: Macmillan, 1916), Chap. 18; and shortcomings of various conceptions of needs are explored in the following: Reginald D. Archambault, "The Concept of Need and Its Relation to Certain Aspects of Educational Theory," *Harvard Educational Review*, **27**, No. 1 (Winter, 1957), pp. 38–62; Paul B. Komisar, " 'Need' and the Needs-Curriculum," in *Language and Concepts in Education*, ed. B. Othanel Smith and Robert H. Ennis (Chicago: Rand McNally, 1961), pp. 24–42.

Man can become fully functioning only after he has sufficiently satisfied the basic needs previously mentioned and thereby provided himself with the freedom to concentrate on fully developing his potentials. Man needs a productive orientation to life. Such an orientation is attained through the use of reason, through productive work in which one can dedicate himself to a meaningful task and express and develop his creative abilities, and through love of another person, all men, and nature, without the loss of integrity and independence.*

It is possible for those who are able to develop their full abilities to be considerably healthier than the society in which they live. Some societies provide more of the conditions that promote psychological health and permit fewer of those that obstruct it, but it should be recognized that all societies, in varying degrees, promote cultural patterns which are inimical to psychological health. Those who find the means to become productive and to develop their abilities in a society that does not often encourage such development must cultivate a certain detachment from their surroundings. This is not an easy task, particularly in light of the fact that there are enormous pressures for conformity in our society. The productive person complies with minor conventions (even with some he may consider foolish) in order to be free to live independently and creatively away from the rabble. He resists only when major principles are at stake.

A healthy society is less repressive than other societies, causes less frustration, and places fewer roadblocks in the way of the full development of its citizens. It is a society in which individuals are less inclined to impose their will in matters of religion, politics, conventions, and other areas; they are more tolerant of the views of others and show greater willingness to give them a fair hearing. A healthy society would not look with suspicion on people who deviate from the common pattern. There would be much greater respect for individual differences and a growing realization that diversity need not be divisive but can be the lifeblood of democracy. Despite much that has been written in the field of education about individual differences, educators all too frequently do not respect and nurture such differences in actual practice. A chief

---

* For a further development of this concept of love, see Erich Fromm, *The Art of Loving* (New York: Harper and Brothers, 1956).

source of difficulty lies in the quality of teachers and administrators, many of whom harbor attitudes that become the nemesis of fruitful cultivation of the unique abilities of students.

Too often societies are erected on forces of power based on the exploitation of the many and the aggrandizement of power for the few. Whenever individuals must live under conditions that exploit them and deny the development of their abilities, they must either succeed in bringing about conditions more in keeping with their needs or perish. Our own society is predicated on the belief that the representative will of the people should establish political, economic, and social conditions that promote human welfare. Societies vary in the extent and the direction of their movement toward the promotion of psychological health. As already mentioned, there are multiple forces in our culture which conflict with the conditions for a healthy society. *"A healthy society furthers man's capacity to love his fellow man, to work creatively, to develop his reason and objectivity, to have a sense of self which is based on the experience of his own productive powers."* * Our concern should be with the direction in which our society presently is moving and the possibilities of bringing it more into line with the characteristics of a healthy society.

Such characteristics would be those which enable men to make full use of their productive abilities. Each individual would benefit from his own and his fellow citizen's development, and society itself would rise to a higher plane. Although no society, present or past, has provided all the conditions needed for full development (and it would be unrealistic to believe that there will be such a society in the future), we can at least move toward a society that attempts, even imperfectly, to nurture such conditions most of the time. A society that attempts to do this would find the needed connections between the past, present, and future, in order to provide continuity. At the same time, however, it would have to attempt to reconstruct on a wide scale those attitudes and social conditions that are favorable to human development. Such a society would also have to be open and flexible so that it could assimilate new knowledge and practices and become sufficiently innovative to avoid rigidity and dogmatism.

---

* Fromm, *The Sane Society*, p. 71. Copyright © 1955 by Erich Fromm; Holt, Rinehart and Winston, Inc., as publishers.

In education, the cultural heritage is the starting point; however, the heritage must always be taught in light of its meaning for present and future life. The mere fact that something has been around for a long time is no reason to revere it—all the more reason to scrutinize it. In order for youth to develop their creative potentials, they need to acquire not a fixed body of knowledge but rather certain attitudes and abilities that will encourage them to pursue lifetime learning. The development of such attitudes and abilities will enable them to explore reflectively the heritage of ideas in diverse fields. And if such explorations are to be fruitful, students and teachers must have the freedom to inquire.

A society imbued with these ideals looks to the future with hope, recognizing that its goal is to become not a static society but rather one whose citizenry is animated by a spirit of continuing achievement.

FOR FURTHER READING

Bluhm, William T. *Theories of the Political System.* Englewood Cliffs, N.J.: Prentice-Hall, 1965.

Boulding, Kenneth E. *The Meaning of The Twentieth Century.* New York: Harper and Row, 1964.

Brameld, Theodore. *Education for the Emerging Age.* New York: Harper and Brothers, 1961.

Brecht, Arnold. *Political Theory: The Foundations of Twentieth Century Political Thought.* Princeton: Princeton University Press, 1959.

Childs, John L. *Education and Morals.* New York: Appleton-Century-Crofts, 1950.

Cremin, Lawrence A. *The Genius of American Education.* New York: Vintage Books, 1966.

Frankel, Charles. *The Democratic Prospect.* New York: Harper and Row, 1962.

Fromm, Erich. *The Sane Society.* Greenwich, Conn.: Fawcett Publications, 1965.

Gardner, John W. *Self-Renewal.* New York: Harper and Row, 1963.

Harrington, Michael. *The Accidental Century.* Baltimore: Penguin Books, 1966.

Henry, Jules. *Culture Against Man.* New York: Random House, 1963.

Kimball, Solon T., and James E. McClellan, Jr. *Education and the New America.* New York: Random House, 1962.

McClelland, David C. *The Achieving Society.* Princeton, N.J.: D. Van Nostrand, 1961.

Michael, Donald N. *The Next Generation.* New York: Vintage Books, 1965.

Riesman, David. *Individualism Reconsidered.* New York: Doubleday, 1965.

Stanley, William O. *Education and Social Integration.* New York: Teachers College, Columbia University, 1953.

Stiles, Lindley J. (ed.). *The Teacher's Role in American Society.* Fourteenth Yearbook of The John Dewey Society. New York: Harper and Brothers, 1957.

Young, Michael. *The Rise of the Meritocracy, 1870–2033.* Baltimore: Penguin Books, 1961.

CHAPTER TWO

ORGANIZATIONAL VALUES AND EDUCATION

Introduction

America has grown from a rural, agrarian country to an urban, industrial one; now we have entered upon a nuclear age, which has wrought vast technological changes that have affected all levels of contemporary life. In order to handle its technological know-how and meet its great economic needs, our country (as well as many other Western industrial nations) has become an organizational society. The industrial revolution, which earlier ushered in an age of new technological procedures derived from the discoveries of modern science, has mechanized and automated industrial processes of production and distribution of goods. Coupled with these changes have been the emergence of powerful labor unions and the growth of big government.

Organizations have proliferated in our society today, organizations of varying size, structures, and purposes to serve the public in their multiple and divergent interests. There are charitable, associational, industrial, governmental, labor, recreational, medical, educational, and other types of organizations. In recent years we have witnessed an increase in the number of large organizations, particularly in industry, labor, government, and education. These include the largest bureaus and subdivisions of government and labor, the 500 largest industrial corporations of America, and the 20 largest universities and public school systems. Face-to-face relations are difficult if not impossible in the huge organizations of today. With the flood of students entering colleges during the 1960's, and with the growth of metropolitan areas and the quickening pace of school district reorganization, both higher education and the public schools have undergone rapid expansion.

PROBLEMS FACED BY EDUCATIONAL ORGANIZATIONS

Educational organizations, like other types of organizations, try to ensure that their basic internal functions operate properly, so that they will be able to attain their goals. After an organization has established its goals, it tries to maintain sufficient control over its operations so that disorganization will not result; and secondly, it attempts to introduce innovations to bring about needed improvements. If the administration is too concerned about control, there may be some suppression of innovative tendencies. On the other hand, if innovation is heavily stressed, the organization may lose considerable control. These two basic functions, the way they operate and the direction they require to work in harmony with one another, will be discussed later.

First, however, it is necessary to examine the way in which authority and power are used. These processes are also related to the establishment of organizational rules for carrying out formal operations in a systematic and consistent fashion and to the use of sanctions to ensure that organizational members fulfill their roles. The success of the organization is considerably affected by the way in which rules and sanctions are used.

Educational organizations have a division of labor based on certain specialties that individuals perform. The quality of personnel performance is evaluated with reference to standards of the specialty. Therefore, in order to be a successful organizational member, an individual must perform well according to the standards relevant to his specialty.

Usually when organizations become large and complex, face-to-face relations among most members are no longer possible. When an organization is small, an informal and commonly understood set of rules can be operative; but with rapid growth in size and complexity, it becomes necessary to initiate a formal and more elaborate set of rules and regulations to govern the multiple functions of the organization. Relations between high administrative authority and personnel become less frequent, in some cases non-existent. Personnel may begin to feel that a "faceless" authority determines their future. This attitude may lead to a feeling of alienation that can endanger the morale of the organization and lead to inefficiency, even to a breakdown in the ability of the organization to achieve its goals.

Such problems can possibly be prevented if the organization takes man's social nature into account by giving individuals the opportunity to have meaningful social contacts and interaction with their peers. Seeing that each person is suited for his position and finds in it a challenge and a sense of growth and fulfillment can be very important. This is a difficult task for industrial management to achieve; perhaps there is a greater likelihood that it can be accomplished in educational institutions. Alienation may also be diminished by involving teaching personnel in decision-making (as in the case of faculty senates in higher education).

We will later explore these problems and ways of remedying them in greater detail, but let us first turn our attention to an examination of organizational models. We will look first at a formal model and then at an informal model.

ORGANIZATIONAL MODELS

Formal Model

One generally associates bureaucracy with officialdom, such as that found in government and industry; usually the epithet "red tape" is used to describe the procedures of officials by those who have been inconvenienced by their meticulous, almost rigid enforcement of rules and regulations. However, this is not the original meaning of "bureaucracy." The term refers to large organizations which are operated on the basis of the principle of efficiency in order to accomplish large-scale administrative tasks. The administrative hierarchy, the system of offices, and the rules and regulations governing their operation are deliberately contrived in order to achieve organizational goals.

The German sociologist Max Weber provided an ideal type or model of a bureaucracy. It is an ideal type in the sense that no actual large organization can completely fulfill the characteristics; nonetheless, an ideal type is useful for purposes of identifying and understanding the formal operations of bureaucracies. The formal operations are those that can be shown in a chart of organizational structure and spelled out in the rules and regulations. Informal activity is not included in such specifications, but its structure can be recognized in the spontaneously formed social groupings of personnel and in the values that they develop toward their work and the administrative hierarchy. We will first consider the formal structure of organizations; we will later examine the informal structure.

The objectives of bureaucracies, according to Weber, are to eliminate irrational and emotional elements, to elevate precision, speed, continuity, unambiguity, and to encourage the subordination of personnel to the administrative hierarchy, in order to reduce friction and keep material and personnel costs at a minimum. In a word, the objective of bureaucratic organizations is efficiency; and organizations that operate in strict accordance with a bureaucratic model seem in general to be more efficient than those that base their operations on some other model.

The manner in which efficiency is maximized and irrational elements are controlled comes from the characteristics of bureaucracies. Following Weber's interpretation,* we note that bureaucracies organize their offices according to the hierarchical principle; in other words, each office is under the supervision and control of a higher one. The lower office has the right to appeal and issue a statement of grievances to the higher one. The manner in which this is done depends on the nature and purpose of the bureaucracy.

Qualifications for each office are specified in writing. The abilities required of the office-holder are delineated, and the official functions to be performed are stipulated. The office is regulated by written rules that serve to designate its limits and to communicate to other members of the bureaucracy the sphere of the office-

---

* See *From Max Weber: Essays in Sociology,* trans. and edited by H. Gerth and C. Wright Mills (New York: Oxford University Press, 1958); Max Weber, *The Theory of Social and Economic Organization,* trans. by A. M. Henderson and Talcott Parsons (New York: Free Press, 1957).

holder's authority. To hold office, one must meet the written standards for qualification; to do so demands specialized training. The objective is to eliminate class privilege in appointments and to ensure that authority will be distributed on the basis of merit, not of wealth or influence. Weber believes that the development of bureaucracy favors the leveling of social classes and, conversely, that all processes of leveling in society create a more favorable atmosphere for the development of bureaucracy.

Employment is based on standards of competence that require specialized training; promotion is based on seniority, achievement, or both. Employment in the system constitutes a career, and the office-holder is protected against arbitrary dismissal. The hierarchical arrangement of offices provides a system of supervision used to evaluate performance, and the system of rules is designed to assure uniform performance of tasks. The office-holder usually has a contractual arrangement with the bureaucracy, and he receives a salary and has a right to a pension. He is expected to perform his duties according to the rules and within his sphere of authority.

The principle of bureaucratic administration is based on the exercise of control through the use of technical knowledge and knowledge gained from experience in the organization. Theoretically, since the most competent persons available fill the positions, utilize their expertise within the framework of the rules, and make evaluations of personnel and operations on this basis, irrational and emotional elements, ambiguity, and friction are reduced to a minimum.

Weber believes that with the rise of modern technology and business methods in the production of goods, bureaucratic administration has become indispensable. In fact, *"When those subject to bureaucratic control seek to escape the influence of the existing bureaucratic apparatus, this is normally possible only by creating an organization of their own which is equally subject to the process of bureaucratization."* *

In the United States, interest in the process of industrial management has led to a number of studies in industry. Fredrick W. Taylor

---

* Weber, *The Theory of Social and Economic Organization*, p. 338. Reprinted with the permission of The Macmillan Company. Copyright 1947 by Talcott Parsons.

advocated the scientific study of jobs based on time-studies of tasks, leading to the establishment of a standard time for each job and payment of wages in proportion to output.* Following Taylor's study, more systematic treatments dealt with the division of labor, specialization and departmentalization of functions, and managerial supervision.†

American businessmen, impressed with the principles of scientific management, pressured public education, from their positions of power on school boards, into adopting industrial management principles in the operation of school systems. The justification for such procedures was greater efficiency and economy.‡

However, the industrial management model is inadequate for educational institutions in many ways. The analogy between industry and education is not close and, when applied too literally, can lead to abuses of the teaching-learning process in the name of efficiency. Only certain aspects of education, such as the business operations of school systems, can operate effectively on this model.

The scientific management approach led to the view that the teacher would be an obedient servant to administrative authority. Bagley held that the teacher's relation to his superiors is analogous to the relation of a man to his superiors in the armed forces, government, and business.§ This outlook came into conflict with emerging ideals of democratic educational administration that arose from the progressive education movement. These ideals for administrator-teacher relations were honored in many cases as an aim rather than a practice. In any case, the clash between scientific management and democratic administration was inevitable so far

---

* Frederick W. Taylor, *Scientific Management* (New York: Harper, 1911).

† James D. Monney and Alan C. Reiley, *Onward Industry* (New York: Harper, 1931). Later published by James D. Monney under the title *The Principles of Organization* (New York: Harper, 1947).

‡ See Raymond E. Callahan, *Education and the Cult of Efficiency* (Chicago: University of Chicago Press, 1962). For a counterthesis see Timothy L. Smith's review of Callahan's book in *History of Education Quarterly*, 4 (March, 1964), pp. 76–77.

§ William Chandler Bagley, *Classroom Management* (New York: Macmillan, 1907).

as their theoretical bases were concerned, even though administrators did not always recognize (in some cases did not want to recognize) their conflict in the actual operation of an educational system.

The formal model of bureaucracy is best used as a tool for viewing the formal structural arrangements of organizations and the interrelationships among the parts of the system. An understanding of human relations in organizations, however, does not come from observation of the formal model alone. It does not show why bureaucracies, although organized to maximize efficiency, are not able to achieve the level of efficiency they seek. The human factor bulks large here; at times it deflects and impedes the process of maximizing efficiency. In order to understand the other factors within an organization that influence the success of the system in achieving its goals, it is necessary to examine an informal model of organizational behavior.

Informal Model

From organizational charts and the formal model alone, one cannot predict organizational effectiveness with a high degree of accuracy; some consideration needs to be given to the influence of human relations in organizations. At the Hawthorne plant of Western Electric Company, Roethlisberger and Dickson made an intensive examination of a shop department and found in operation certain informal group structures.* A number of cliques, with their own leadership structure, served as instruments of control that influenced work production and attitudes toward management. These groupings arose out of day-to-day activities as men sought expression of their need for personal relationships that management did not provide. The bases for informal groupings were friendship ties, acceptance by others, and factors of prestige. The groups took on the characteristics of a power relationship by exerting control over their members and influencing their mode of work and their productive output.

Informal groups do not appear on organizational charts; they arise more or less spontaneously to satisfy social and economic needs

---

* F. J. Roethlisberger and W. J. Dickson, *Management and the Worker* (Cambridge: Harvard University Press, 1941).

that are not met by the formal organizational structure. According to Barnard, the functions of informal structures within the formal organization are:

1)　provision of a means of communication by which norms of conduct between superordinates and subordinates are established and reinforced,

2)　"maintenance of cohesiveness in formal organizations through regulating the willingness to serve and the stability of objective authority,"

3)　"maintenance of the feeling of personal integrity, of self-respect, of independent choice." *

So far it has been stated that informal groups arise in response to social needs; at this point, however, more can be said about the factors that influence their development. In order for a long-term group to develop, it is necessary that individuals have frequent face-to-face contact. The physical characteristics of the organization are important here, for those who work close to one another will have more opportunities to form such relationships.† Coupled with this is the factor of occupation: those performing similar jobs are more likely to associate with one another in an informal group arrangement. There will still be differences of interest, even among those who have similar jobs and work in close proximity to one another, thereby leading to the emergence of special interest groups. From time to time in any large organization, special issues arise that are of concern to many members of the organization. There is a tendency for those of divergent interests, occupations, and locations of work within the organization to form a group to deal with the issue. After the issue is settled, men resume their earlier informal group attachments; in certain instances, however, the group established in response to the special issue may develop into a more formal group (as in the case of unions or teacher organizations).

Informal groups are regulated by unwritten norms established by leaders and members, or, at times, only by those in leadership

---

* C. I. Barnard, *The Functions of the Executive* (Cambridge: Harvard University Press, 1940), pp. 122–123.

† Leon Festinger, Stanley Schachter, and Kurt Back, *Social Pressures in Informal Groups* (New York: Harper and Brothers, 1950), pp. 153–163.

positions. These groups often revise the job expectations declared by those in positions of authority in the formal organization, with the result that the amount of work and the manner in which it is performed are controlled by group norms. Informal systems of communication within these groups, commonly known as the "grapevine," frequently spread word of official policy before it has been announced by formal organizational authority.

Organizations at all levels, whether they deal in a product or service or perform a specialized welfare function for society, are known to have informal groups. The need to establish such groups is said to arise for social reasons, since man must find in his work more than just an economic gain. Mayo believed that man finds his basic sense of identity through his social relations; the social influences of the informal group strike a more responsive chord in workers than do the incentives and directives of management. The worker is likely to be responsive to management to the extent that the supervisor can meet the subordinate's need for acceptance.* A number of studies in business and industry indicate that social relations through informal group membership affect productivity, quality of work, job satisfaction and morale.† Those in positions of authority, then, can ill afford to ignore the informal groups and their expectations if organizational goals are to be pursued successfully. In conclusion, both the formal and informal models of organizational operations are needed for a more complete understanding of organizational processes.

ORGANIZATIONAL PROCESSES

Organizational Goals

In general, bureaucratic organizations are considered better able than are other types of organizations to maximize efficiency and thus to achieve organizational goals with the least expenditure of

---

* Elton Mayo, *The Social Problems of an Industrial Civilization* (Boston: Harvard Business School, 1945).

† See A. Zalesnik, C. R. Christensen, and F. J. Roethlisberger, *The Motivation, Productivity, and Satisfaction of Workers: A Prediction Study* (Boston: Div. of Research, Harvard Business School, 1958); W. F. Whyte, *Human Relations in the Restaurant Industry* (New York: McGraw-Hill, 1948).

resources. Sometimes new organizations are developed to fulfill goals that are not being achieved or have not been achieved sufficiently by existing organizational structures.

Both general and specific goals can be found in organizations. General goals are usually considered the *raison d'être* for the organization's existence. Specific goals may be subsumed under general goals; they are formulated to guide the various departments and subdivisions within the organizational structure.

The overall objective of any educational system is to provide the finest education possible with the resources and personnel in the system. Some of the general goals of educational programs are promotion of worthy use of leisure time; development of effective citizenship; encouragement of critical and reflective thinking abilities; and provision of knowledge and understanding of the cultural heritage. Specific goals in educational programs could be the ability to handle the multiplication table; knowledge of the events that led up to the Revolutionary War; ability to compute interest on loans; and skill in conjugating irregular French verbs.

A number of problems may be encountered in handling organizational goals. General goals may be formulated in such abstract and ideal terms that personnel may be unable to determine whether certain activities help to accomplish or obstruct them. Organizations also are not always effective in their systems of communication; this may lead to a lack of understanding of goals in relationship to work tasks. In fact, industrial workers gear their activities to the more specific goals of their divisions and to the goals and norms found within their informal group structure. One task of the administrator is to see that the goals of the various departments accord with and promote the goals of the organization as a whole. Supervisors and administrators must work with informal groups in an effort to align their direction with the goals of the formal organization. Since the goals of workers in industry may not coincide with those of management, it is necessary for management to offer material incentives and rewards for performing prescribed tasks well.

Bureaucratic organization tends to heighten rationality. Whenever those involved in decision-making processes share the same operational goals, disagreements are settled by examining the consequences of alternative courses of action; however, when goals are not shared, as in the case of management and the worker, differences are settled by bargaining.

As the members of an organization come to agree firmly on goals, there is an increase in the tendency to become involved and identified with the organization. These members will probably strive to be considered assets to the organization and will make an effort to comply with the rules. Their behavior will tend to conform more to the expectations of those in authority. And as their commitment to the organization grows, they experience increasing frustration whenever the goals of the organization are thwarted.

Bureaucratic organizations may pursue several goals simultaneously. The more complex the organization becomes, the more difficult it is to recognize specific goals and reconcile conflict between them. In order to avoid some of these problems, an attempt may be made to make goals operational. Goals expressed in terms of the types of organizational behavior they signify are called "operational." But whether a goal is expressed operationally is not always an "either-or" question, since operationality is a matter of degree. In any case, members are better able to see how a course of action will promote goal realization when goals are expressed in operational terms.

There is always the danger of goal displacement in large organizations. Displacement occurs whenever means used to attain goals become ends in themselves. Some functionaries may glorify routine patterns and prescribed forms of organizational behavior for their own sake rather than for their intended purpose. For example, the filing of countless forms in triplicate may be a sacred domain ruled by a minor functionary, who has elevated the practice to an end in itself. This may be one reason why the public seldom sees bureaucracies as efficient, economical, and successful in their operations. Rather, they are depicted as overladen with "red tape," impersonal and curt in their relations with the public, and even inefficient and wasteful.

Organizations face a number of problems in establishing and carrying out their goals successfully. A common one, disagreement on goals, is encountered whenever the staff of a school system places certain general goals ahead of the official goals formulated by the school district. This situation can be seen in Peabody's study of an elementary school. He found that the goals toward which teachers were working did not coincide in weight and importance with those officially promulgated by the school district.* When this occurs, open conflict is likely to ensue and school district officials and teachers confront one another over the discrepancy. Disruptive conflict can usually be avoided if teachers are willing to accede to the demands of the administration. If each group insists that its own position be upheld, then procedures should be established to permit all parties, fairly and impartially, to air their grievances and express their thinking on the matter, and measures should be provided for adjudicating the conflict in an amicable manner. Although authority is somewhat delegated in all organizations, it is more extensively delegated in educational and other organizations that employ professionals or semiprofessionals, because persons of greater competence are usually given larger roles in decision-making. Industrial workers do not customarily participate in formulating goals for industrial concerns; their voices have little effect on the profit motive of industry or on decisions about distribution of profits. The position of management, however, has been strongly countered by the rise of powerful labor unions. Even if workers do not agree on the goals established by management, they are able, when their unions are strong, to bargain for the material remuneration and incentives that will encourage them to work toward managerial goals.

But are material gains enough to induce workers to help the organization meet production quotas in order to maximize profits? We have seen that all organizations have an informal network of voluntary social relations that cannot be found on official organizational charts. These informal groups arise to meet needs not satisfied by those in positions of authority, and administrative authority cannot eradicate them, for if forcibly disbanded, they would be replaced by others, operating surreptitiously if necessary. Even short of attempting to eradicate informal groups, administrative authority will probably discover that considerable pressure on them may bring about a drop in the rate of production, increased absenteeism, a higher accident rate, etc. Management must work with and through them; their cooperation must be solicited. Men not only desire material gain from their work; they also seek some form of social relationship and some measure of social fulfillment.

---

* Robert L. Peabody, *Organizational Authority* (New York: Atherton Press, 1965), pp. 74–76.

In terms of individual behavior and the choice and pursuit of goals, Rotter's principal contention is that human behavior depends on:

1)   the degree to which a person expects the behavior to have a successful outcome,

2)   the value of that success to the person trying to achieve it.*

Administrative authorities should then be aware that, theoretically at least, a person will not try very earnestly to reach a goal he does not value, no matter how certain he is that he can obtain it; he may try very hard, on the other hand, even with little hope of success, if he does value the goal enough. Consequently, the problem of organizations that have traditionally relied on material inducements to get personnel to help achieve goals, is one of developing better *esprit de corps* within the organization. By using modern techniques to persuade personnel to identify their goals with those of the organization, administrators may find they need to rely less on material rewards and the sanction and support of informal group relations.

In contrast to the more univocal goals found in industry, the goals of educational systems vary greatly. There are considerable differences in the goals of public, private, and parochial school systems, and some differences exist between individual public schools. Goals formulated for a school system are usually something less than ideal, because educators must consider the limits of institutional realities, the resources available, and the demands and restrictions imposed upon schools by the local community.

In the United States today we are not altogether sure whether our primary aim is liberal education or vocational preparation, whether we wish to prepare youth for appreciating the world of scholarship or for fulfilling the duties of citizenship. As a consequence, school systems diverge widely in their aims.

Educational systems face the problem of formulating their general goals operationally so that teachers will know the types of behavior and conditions they need to bring about for goal fulfillment. There is a problem of articulating the specific goals in the separate subject areas with general goals. The teacher needs to know in

---

* Julian B. Rotter, *Social Learning and Clinical Psychology* (Englewood Cliffs, N.J.: Prentice-Hall, 1954).

what way the goals established for his area of the curriculum relate to and promote the general goals. All too often this relationship is not clearly defined, and there is a resulting lack of coordination in the program and a sense of ambiguity concerning the ways that separate efforts contribute to overall outcomes that promote realization of general goals.*

Therefore, the effectiveness of goals in guiding educational programs is directly related to the provisions that administrators and teachers make to ensure their effectiveness. We have shown how goals influence various organizational functions and how these functions influence both the formulation and the use of goals. Another question of an entirely different nature can be raised: "What goals should American schools adopt?" This is basically a philosophical question, equivalent to: "What educational values are of greatest worth?" It could be turned into an empirical question by deciding that the information for its answer could be gained from a public opinion poll designed to tell us which goals the public considers most desirable. Yet more than this is surely needed, for there is also the question as to who should determine the goals of education. Should it be teachers, administrators, school board members, the public, or some combination of these? Even if the goals of education can be determined by empirical methods, there remains the question as to whether they should be so determined. The question is philosophical in nature because an adequate answer must be based on an understanding of the purpose of the school in a democratic society.

At times, when asking about the goals that American schools should adopt, the questioner is presumably seeking enlightenment of a different nature. He is asking for criteria by which goals can be evaluated. Goals are sometimes derived from a philosophy of education in the sense that the philosophy serves as a model for certain ideal goals, but they are frequently generated by institutions and agencies of the larger society. In some cases a philosophy of education may serve to primarily rationalize, systematize, or criticize goals that it did not create. Whenever goals are derived from a philosophy of education, however, it becomes appropriate

---

* For further discussion of educational goals and instructional objectives, see Benjamin S. Bloom (ed.), *Taxonomy of Educational Objectives*, 2 vols. (New York: Longmans, Green, 1956, 1964).

to inquire which philosophy is best? Criteria for this type of evaluation must come, not from one philosophy, but from various ones, independently of each other for purposes of appraisal. Criteria derived from within a single philosophy might show only that the particular philosophy fulfills the criteria and therefore might lead to the questionable conclusion that this philosophy is the best one to use in establishing goals for educational systems.

The enormous task of developing such criteria by comparing the various philosophies would divert us from our central purpose of making at least an initial appraisal of desirable educational goals. One way to deal with the problem is to note, first of all, that education, as part of a larger democratic society, has certain obligations if it is to serve the society in a manner consistent with democratic principles. Much has been written about the meaning of a democratic education, and during the progressive education movement it was believed, among other things, that such an education involved teacher-pupil planning and the joint formulation of educational policy by teachers and administrators. However, there are still matters open to question in this area. What, indeed, is the most desirable relationship between teachers and pupils, between teachers and administrators? Is joint planning on various levels merely desirable, or do such practices stem directly from the nature of a democratic education?

At this point at least two principles of democratic education should perhaps be enunciated: equality of educational opportunity and academic freedom for teachers and students. Our history is tied closely to the conviction that a democracy cannot survive without an educated citizenry. Closely associated with our democratic ideals is the principle of equality of educational opportunity. Various interpretations of this principle can be found in the educational literature; this discussion is itself an interpretation.

Some people state that all men are equal and then seek to substantiate this principle by mistakenly looking for fundamental characteristics that seem to make all men alike. To such persons "equal" suggests the same physical size or the same I.Q. Theoretically, measuring instruments could determine whether two or more persons are alike. If they are, they might be given the same educational opportunities, be enrolled in the same curriculum, and have the same teachers.

But this seems to be an erroneous way to handle the principle. Not only are we aware that persons differ greatly in intellectual, emotional, and physical characteristics, but the principle of equality cannot be enunciated in strictly descriptive terms. Equality of educational opportunity is a prescriptive principle, customarily used to prescribe certain actions or policies. What is prescribed varies as the context changes from race to sex to juvenile delinquency, to still another problem. In a prescriptive interpretation of equality it is important that the practices chosen be consistent with previously formulated rules which are correctly applied to the persons being considered. The rules may encompass nondiscrimination on racial or religious grounds, or they may relate to the educational treatment of the handicapped or retarded child. Most students are already acquainted with rules applying the equality principle to admission practices of colleges and of graduate and professional schools. One may question, however, whether the rules themselves are sound. To meet this test, rules must be based on certain moral or ethical principles. For example, if there is no discrimination, whether overt or tacit, because of race in college admission practices, then they are apparently based on the principle that racial discrimination in education is morally wrong.

To state the equality principle negatively: persons are not to be differentially treated unless there are relevant and sufficient reasons for doing so. The justification for differential treatment can be determined by examining the rules applicable in the context to see if they are being applied correctly. Occasionally the rules themselves will be questioned, as previously indicated, by means of an evaluation of the ethical principles on which the rules are based. Thus, one can investigate a claim that equality of educational opportunity has been denied by examining the particular situation with reference to the rules which govern the context in order to reveal whether differential treatment was justified. If the rules were applied correctly, then the matter presumably could be settled—unless someone seriously questioned the adequacy of one or more of the ethical principles underlying the rules.

Academic freedom for teachers and students, another essential principle of democratic education, is the freedom to pursue truth and to seek knowledge in any area of human experience. Academic freedom includes the right to question, analyze, and criticize our most cherished beliefs and institutions, including our belief in the value of freedom of inquiry itself. The pursuit of learning proceeds best when it is unfettered.

Responsibilities, however, accompany these freedoms. The teacher must not pose as an authority outside his area of competence; he must not inject into his teaching irrelevant material which exceeds the logical boundaries of his course; he must be open to the inquiries of others even when they conflict with his own beliefs; and he has a responsibility to alter his beliefs whenever evidence proves them faulty. The teacher must necessarily learn to recognize his own point of view in order that he may be able to present all sides of a controversial issue fairly.

Why should we support academic freedom? First there is the fact that many contributions to our society, in both the arts and the sciences, would probably have been impossible had academic freedom been denied. In other words, one can support academic freedom simply on the grounds that society has benefited from it and would be the worse without the achievements it has fostered. However, academic freedom can also be jusified by its relationship with democracy, which depends on knowledgeable and informed citizens to make intelligent decisions. Academic freedom, together with freedom of speech and of the press, is necessary if a democratic society is to develop an intelligent and informed citizenry. Therefore, if one accepts democracy as preferable to other social and political arrangements, one must recognize that academic freedom is a necessary condition for its sustenance.

Educational goals in a democratic society must be consonant with the principles of a democratic education. The principles of equality of educational opportunity and academic freedom for teachers and students are necessary conditions for educational goals to fulfill. No doubt other principles will come to mind. At this point, however, we need to turn our attention to other aspects of organizational operations.

Organizational Control

All organizations face the problem of maintaining sufficient control and direction over their operations to enable them to achieve their goals. Whenever control over operations is lost, a state of disorganization is likely to ensue. Organizations that follow a bureaucratic model are likely to try at all costs to avoid disorganization. Since innovation is likely to cause some temporary disruptions, an organization wishing to bring about needed changes will have to permit greater toleration for temporary states of disorganization. Resolution of the problem, then, becomes the decision as to what conditions giving rise to an unsettled state can be sanctioned by those in authority, and how far such conditions can be permitted to develop before organizational controls are imposed.

Although all organizations must exercise control over their operations, it is important to note how such control is imposed. Some forms of control may be undesirable. Whenever the system of controls becomes so rigid that it precludes innovation, the system itself needs modification. For it is a basic principle that sooner or later an organization will have to innovate in order to achieve its goals—and all innovations diverge in some manner from practices previously established and brought under some degree of organizational control. Neither should we conclude that all innovation is desirable, however. From the point of view of the administrative hierarchy, the test of an innovation is its power to enable the organization to attain its goals in the most economical manner possible. But since the goals of personnel may not coincide with official goals, the test of an innovation or of the control process will not necessarily be the same for employees as for the administration.

Thus solution to the problem of control lies in getting personnel to identify their goals with those of the organization, for whenever this occurs, problems of control are reduced to a minimum. But, as we have seen earlier, workers have social needs as well as economic ones, and whenever the organization ignores social needs or impedes their fulfillment, problems of control are likely to result.

Organizations utilize various means to bring about control. Certain aspects of control inhere in a generalized deference to authority. Those in positions of power, through their offices and titles, are likely to receive some degree of respect for and compliance with their directives. Their formal roles or positions in the administrative hierarchy create an aura or respect and deference among those who hold lower positions in the organization.

Respect for authority and formal role position, however, is not always sufficient as a basis for control. In some cases the administrative official is recognized not only by the status his office confers upon him, but also by his competence, his technical know-how and expertise in a particular area. In other words, personnel may tend to denigrate an office if they consider the official incompetent; but whenever he can display technical competence based on specialized knowledge, an additional factor of respect is generated and probably along with it a greater willingness to carry out the official's decisions.

In many cases the personality of the official has an effect on control. If he is skillful in human relations and can effectively employ techniques of persuasion rather than coercion, personnel are more likely to carry out their functions in the prescribed manner. The skillful official usually relates successfully to members of the organization by showing an appreciative awareness of their needs and problems. Once in a great while a leader of unusually persuasive qualities acquires in the eyes of subordinates a charismatic quality that inspires remarkable acts of dedication and loyalty on their part. But such instances are uncommon, and most of those in leadership positions need to establish support for their policies through the respect accorded the authority of their offices, through expertise, through human relations skill, or some combination of these factors.

After organizational objectives are established, officials must determine policies and rules for the organization, plans for attaining the objectives, and methods for implementing the plans. Rules are developed in order that organizational plans may move smoothly toward the attainment of objectives. Rules prescribe desired forms of procedure in utilizing resources and carrying out work tasks and for personnel interrelationships within the organization. A system of sanctions, embracing rewards and punishments, is developed to encourage personnel to perform their tasks and conduct themselves according to rule specifications. The rewards may be prizes, honors, recognition, and material awards; punishments may range from criticism to dismissal. Sanctions lose much of their effectiveness if it is possible to violate rules wthout detection or, on the other hand, if good performance goes unrewarded. It is also true that rules remain effective only when they are enforced in a fair and impartial manner; exceptions should be made only in unusual cases, and even then only with adequate justification for the lack of uniformity.

Etzioni classifies organizations by type of authority or power used; the type of authority becomes the dominant mode of control.* The forms of authority are coercive, utilitarian, normative, and mixed. Coercive authority is the predominant characteristic of concentration camps, prisons, prisoner-of-war camps, custodial mental institutions, and some unions; utilitarian authority, based on the use of economic rewards, is found usually in business and industry, business unions, farmers' organizations, and peacetime military organizations; normative authority, based on membership, status, and intrinsic value rewards, is found in religious organizations, ideologically based political organizations, hospitals, colleges and universities, social unions, and voluntary and professional associations; and mixed forms of authority can be found in combat units (normative-coercive), most labor unions (utilitarian-normative), and some early industries, farms, company towns, and ships (utilitarian-coercive).

We have discussed modes of authority in business and industry, which are based primarily on economic rewards, and we have seen that in a number of cases other factors, such as consideration of social needs and the cultivation of effective human relations between management and workers, are also necessary to maintain control and thereby ensure that goals will be attained. Our concern here, however, is with the use of normative authority in educational organizations.

Personal qualities of administrators are more important in educational systems than in organizations that rely primarily on coercion. Educational organizations attempt to secure desired leadership qualities in administrators, and an educational system with such leaders is less likely to find its leadership localized in informal groups than is the case in utilitarian and coercive organizations.

There are several factors which bear on sound control:

1)   adequate formal education for professionals,

2)   selection of qualified personnel,

3)   a sound in-service training program designed to acquaint new personnel with the operations and expectations of the system and to ensure that their competence is maintained at a desired level.

---

* A. Etzioni, *A Comparative Analysis of Complex Organizations* (Glencoe, Ill.: Free Press, 1961).

The process implied in the first factor—that of providing a sound formal education—is not the function of public school systems, although they indirectly affect that process by their choice of teachers. The process of selecting qualified persons depends an the early recruitment of able young people for educational careers and the quality of their formal educational program. With the mushrooming of school enrollments in recent years, the demand for qualified people in certain fields has exceeded the supply. The selection process is also guided by a judicious appraisal of the candidate's characteristics in relation to the educational needs of the system. As new personnel enter the system, they need to be introduced to the program and the expected and prescribed ways of behavior by means of a system of indoctrination or inculcation. Finally, as part of in-service work, periodic opportunities are needed for improving competence.

If any stage of the sequence described above fails to function effectively, it will prove difficult for a normative system of controls to operate successfully. Normative control is best used with professionals; consequently, if the system has recruited persons who lack professional competence and a professional outlook toward their responsibilities, organizational authority is more likely to have to take the form of utilitarian control, or some combination of utilitarian and normative control. The result is essentially the same whether the relatively unprofessional recruits were selected for the system because of inadequate criteria of appraisal or because of a limited budget.

Ultimately, however, the normative basis for judging any educational system is the quality of the education it provides for its students. Thus, all controls should be directed toward operating the system in such a manner that the desired ends can be achieved.

Finally, it is necessary, through in-service programs, to provide professionals with a knowledge of the system and to offer opportunities for them to maintain and improve their competence. It is important, however, not to place too many rules and regulations in the way of professionals. Since they are best qualified to determine desirable practices in their specialties, they can perform at a high level and continue to grow in professional competence only when they enjoy the freedom to use their abilities in ways they have themselves chosen after careful evaluation and appraisal. This does not mean that professionals are a law unto themselves; they still must abide by the general rules and regulations of the organization and see to it that their activities contribute in some manner to the realization of organizational goals. What is needed, however, is freedom by those best qualified to judge the way in which specific tasks are to be handled; in other words, the administration should give professionals a "free hand" to use their abilities and judgment so long as this does not result in conflict with organizational policy. Conflicts will inevitably arise, and when they do, educational organizations must allow for the airing of grievances and the reassessment of policies. Only in this manner can the conflicts be discussed by all concerned parties in order that a course of action may be taken to improve conditions.

The problem the administration confronts in regulating the professional arises from the fact that the professional is best qualified to judge what needs to be done in his area and how it should be done. Consequently, the administration may face conflict whenever it attempts to provide extensive supervision of the activities of professionals. Teachers in many public schools are not treated as professionals in this respect, for they are extensively supervised and given directives on the carrying out of their tasks. In addition, they are expected to perform many tasks, such as collecting milk funds, taking up tickets, etc., that are not directly related to teaching.

Although the administration is not strictly qualified to judge how a professional should perform his tasks, most administrators would not willingly relinquish evaluation altogether. They still wish to determine the performance of personnel. One way they do this is to look, not at the performance of the tasks themselves, but at the results—the end product of the performance. Records can be kept on the graduates of an institution to see how successful they are in later life. But such an approach is fraught with the difficulty of separating from one another the many influences on the life of a student in order to pinpoint the influence that one teacher had. The problem is more commonly handled by asking for student evaluation of teachers or by studying student performance on various standardized tests. Factors such as student maturity and the validity of the evaluation instrument must be considered if the former method is used. If standardized tests are used, the validity of the measuring instrument is again important, but another factor is the extent to which class work consisted of drills by the teacher to ensure that his students would score high. In any case, the problems besetting the administration in making accurate and reliable evaluations of professionals are serious indeed. Administrators would prefer more tangible and less ambiguous ways of evaluating, such as the practice in major universities of using the professor's record on research and publications as a primary basis for evaluation.

In terms of "line and staff," professionals are not treated as lower ranks on the line of the administrative hierarchy, but as staff, outside the chain of command and with a certain measure of autonomy. Although carrying no administrative authority, the staff can advise the administration on various policies, particularly those that have direct bearing on themselves. The staff also can exercise authority in limited areas that relate in some manner to their tasks, and they can direct and supervise personnel who assist them in their professional work. The division of authority tends to break down when problems fall into both line and staff spheres of jurisdiction; and in the process of deciding which group has authority in a particular case, those lower in rank can play one group against the other. The center of conflict, according to Dalton, is the tendency of the higher and lower line personnel to form a coalition against the staff.* However, in professional organizations, such as those formed primarily to perform a research function, administrators are usually in charge of secondary activities, and the professional makes his own professional decisions. In the research organization, for example, he decides what research he will undertake. Actually, some researchers affiliate with large universities that have excellent research facilities in preference to private research organizations. Even though such a choice may be less lucrative, it offers the greater freedom of university research.

At the present time educational institutions employ both professionals and semiprofessionals. Professionals are more likely to be found at the most prestigious universities, while elementary teachers could, in general, be characterized as semiprofessionals. Although semiprofessionals have less autonomy than professionals and are under greater control of the administration (as is evidenced in many elementary schools and in a number of secondary schools),

---

* Melville Dalton, "Conflicts between Staff and Line Managerial Officers," *American Sociological Review*, **15** (1950), pp. 342–351.

they still enjoy greater autonomy than do white- or blue-collar workers. Semiprofessionals are involved primarily in the communication of knowledge rather than in the creation of new knowledge; and in this respect their qualities are compatible with administration. The semiprofessional, in contrast to the professional, is more likely to use his teaching position and educational experience as a ladder of promotion to administrative positions. This procedure has been particularly characteristic of married men with families who go into public school teaching.

Today the typical professional is male, whereas the semiprofessional is more likely to be female. Women have been discouraged from pursuing professional careers for a multitude of reasons. The acceptance of women into medicine and university teaching has been limited. Some administrators may prefer women in semiprofessional positions because of their allegedly greater amenability to administrative control; it should be recognized, however, that there are wide variations in amenability to control that transcend sex, and any theory designed to deal with this problem adequately must take such factors into account.

Two terms that help explain comparative factors involved in organizational control are "pervasiveness" and "scope." * Pervasiveness refers to the extent of the activities that the norms attempt to control. The greater the range of activities an organization controls, the more pervasive it is. For example, a municipal nonresidential university extends its control only to the student's academic life and is consequently less pervasive than a boarding school, whose control is not limited to the academic but extends to most aspects of the student's life. Of course, problems increase as an organization extends its control over a wider range of the student's life. Today, for example, there is disagreement between students and administration in our residential colleges and universities over the areas and the extent of administrative regulation of the lives of students.

"Scope" refers to the number of activities carried on jointly by organizational members. The more activities members engage in together, the broader the scope. Probably maximum scope is found

---

* See Amitai Etzioni, *Modern Organizations* (Englewood Cliffs, N.J.: Prentice-Hall, 1964), pp. 70–74.

in convents and prisons. Returning to our comparison of the non-residential university and the boarding school, we can see that scope is broader in the latter. Since most activities in residential institutions take place on campus, members are more shielded from outside organizations and any counterinfluence they may exert. Clearly an educational organization attempting to develop a certain type of person will have greater opportunity to do so if the scope of the organization is wide. We have seen that the more pervasive an organization attempts to be, the greater the range of control it must exert. In some cases organizations develop norms to regulate the conduct of its members even when the members do not participate jointly in activities. This serves to multiply the number of activities an organization supervises and, since every organization is limited as to how far it can extend its control, to weaken its effectiveness and to lessen its ability to get members to abide by its norms. Thus, pervasiveness and scope are not identical.

Finally, it should be noted that the effectiveness of normative controls in educational organizations depends on the recruitment, selection, and employment of highly qualified professionals. Normative controls are based on status, prestige, appeals to professional ideals, and the intrinsic value of one's work. If a candidate is not fully qualified as a professional he will not respond to an appeal to professional ideals as a method of maintaining organizational control. Wherever educational personnel are more semi-professional than professional in their qualifications, mixed forms of controls, such as normative-utilitarian, will be necessary. Utilitarian controls in educational organizations would take the form of material rewards and security. Since traditionally teaching has been conspicuously lacking in attractive material rewards, however, the emphasis has fallen on security, with tenure provisions as its principal feature. The necessity for tenure to protect academic freedom and to ensure that controversial issues can be discussed in the classroom has been championed many times in the past. Yet tenure has been criticized for, among other reasons, its tendency to attract those seeking primarily security rather than an adventure of the mind. By the very nature of their motivations, professionals seek their reward in the intrinsic excitement of their work and in the opportunity to develop their abilities along lines they have chosen to pursue. Apparently, then, educational organizations may need to use mixed forms of controls at levels where semiprofessionals are employed, whereas with professionals, appeals to codes of ethics, status, prestige, competency, and pride in work are more likely to bring about control. However, certain administrative policies are interpreted at times as violations or infringements on professional responsibilites. Years of struggle and debate have led to greater participation by faculty in policy-making at the college and university level. Faculty senates have experienced mixed success in gaining a greater role in policy formation; however, the trend seems to be toward greater participation in decision-making in the immediate future. Public school teachers, because of the greater militancy of their educational associations in recent years, have gained a larger voice in the affairs of their system than they earlier enjoyed. As educational associations gain greater strength and wider support, teachers are likely to find themselves in a better bargaining position. At all levels of education, trends seem to point to greater shared responsibility in the future.

Control by Commands and Prescriptions

There are three general forms of discourse by which those in authority attempt to regulate the actions of teachers: imperatives; persuasion and psychological techniques; and prescriptions based on evaluations. Let us put forward the hypothesis that the higher the qualifications and the more professionally minded the teacher, the less effective the first two approaches will be in exercising control over faculty; that they are more likely, instead, to engender conflict and dissatisfaction between teachers and administrators; and that prescriptions based on evaluations or value judgments are more likely to bring out improvements in educational practices. Let us examine first the characteristics of imperatives.

Imperatives are commands that administrators sometimes use in order to get a teacher, a certain group of teachers, or the entire faculty to carry out a specified set of activities. Such commands usually take the imperative form (e.g., "Turn in all grades by 5:00 p.m."). One's peers may issue commands, but with no authority behind them, such commands have little force and it is unlikely that they will be obeyed. Commands gain their force not only from the status vested in a position of authority over others, but from the capacity of the incumbent to use sanctions to see that the command is obeyed.

However, one cannot legitimately order a teacher to carrry out a certain task if he is incapable of doing so. If the task is beyond the teacher's ability, whether physical or intellectual, then a command to do it would be unreasonable. If the task calls for procedures that are presently beyond the teacher's ability yet within range of his capacity to acquire at a future date, then the command will be justifiable only if it allows for the time factor. If the statement is made that, "All elementary teachers in the school system will instruct children in the new math," then ample time to develop needed competence must be given if some of the teachers involved have not already acquired it.

But administrators in general are less likely today than formerly to use many imperatives; they are more inclined to use persuasion and psychological techniques to effect compliance with their policies. Some of these techniques and the language of persuasion too often lead to the manipulation of persons, reflecting a view of teachers as interchangeable cogs in a giant machine. Those in the hierarchy sometimes mask such questionable practices and attitudes under the rubric "democratic administration" and succeed thereby in intimidating the insecure and the docile. From their point of view, it would help to recruit enough of these people to assure that policies meet little resistance and are faithfully executed.

But from highly qualified, professionally minded teachers imperatives and psychological techniques are likely to meet with considerable resistance. They may, in fact, generate discord within the system. The well-qualified teacher usually feels that he has the abilities and inner resources to wrestle successfully with the diverse and complex situations which he daily confronts. Yet, viewing himself as a professional and a specialist in his field, he is willing to approach complex situations by conducting rational discussions and evaluations of teaching with the administration. On the basis of these discussions, the teacher is willing to listen to prescriptive statements made by administrators and consider them on their merits.

Prescriptive statements are recommendations; the person addressed is free to decide whether to follow the prescription or to reject it. An example is: You should try using ability groupings. A prescriptive statement is not an empirical statement. An empirical statement provides information that can be verified or refuted. Example: Three elementary schools in the district are using ability groupings. To prescribe, to make recommendations, is to engage in a rational practice; the one to whom the recommendation is given can always ask for the justification and the grounds on which it is based. With commands it is not legitimate to do so. A prescriptive statement is a value judgment that contextually implies that one has engaged in a reasoning process before making the recommendation. The reasoning process may have been conducted carefully and rigorously, or a decision may have been reached with a minimum of careful thought. If little thought has gone into the prescription, then it will prove difficult to support if its justification is asked for.

When one asks for justification of a prescription, empirical statements will constitute some part of the answer. If one asks, for example, why he should use ability groupings in the classroom, the person making the recommendation may cite empirical studies indicating results of the use of ability groupings. But empirical data alone are never entirely sufficient as justification of a prescription. One must determine through rules of relevance whether the data apply to the situation under consideration and also decide whether the use of ability groupings would be in keeping with educational objectives (which are normative considerations).

Thus it seems that when administrators deal with well-qualified professionals, the dialogue used to get teachers to perform certain acts should take the form of prescriptions. Since prescriptions are based on value judgments that, presumably, are rationally conceived, they can be defended and analyzed, as needed. Whenever this level of discourse is used, a rational dialogue can usually be promoted.

The Innovative Process

Educational organizations develop policies and methods of operation to control and coordinate their activities. While existing policies are moving the organization ahead successfully, major innovations are unlikely to be introduced. (Innovations will be projected for the future, however, if provisions for long-term planning are systematically included within the organizational structure.) Educational organizations have had a tendency to resist innovations for a number of reasons. First of all, it is easier for personnel to continue to operate as they have done in the past than to adapt themselves to innovations and learn the new skills that such innovations may demand. Furthermore, the administration may have to compromise on desired innovations because they believe the present staff incapable of carrying out new programs successfully. Second, citizens tend to revere older programs of education—particularly those remembered from their own school days. This form of conservatism encourages school systems to eschew any marked departures from existing programs. Third, there is the problem of finance. Since new programs usually call for additional expenditures or the shifting of funds from older programs, resistance is likely to be encountered unless a skillful public relations campaign is undertaken. Since any new program places a greater demand on institutional resources, the organization may gravitate toward a state of inaction, which absorbs no additional resources.

Of course, not every change in an organization can be considered an innovation. Many changes are related to existing policies designed to coordinate and control the organization's operations. Output in a factory can change for a number of reasons that are not the result of a consciously contrived innovation. In schools there are changes from time to time in the behavior of administrators, teachers, and students in relation to the ongoing operation of the system. Innovations, however, are not just changes in the carrying out of daily operations and the role expectations of the system. Rather, innovations are deliberately contrived attempts to bring about changes in the organization in certain directions that are deemed desirable. Thus, although all innovations effect changes in the organization, not all changes can rightfully be considered innovations.

There are those who fear innovations, either because they believe present practices adequate, or because a change of any kind constitutes a psychological threat to them. On the other hand, there are those who believe that we live in a rapidly changing world that places heavy demands on education to keep pace; such persons usually have a positive attitude toward innovations and seek to bring them about. We cannot evaluate these two points of view;

we can only assess the innovations themselves, either planned or undertaken. In other words, the desirability of innovations depends on the effects they have within a particular organization. To make such an assessment one would need to know the organization's goals, its existing program for attaining them, the basis on which the innovations have been justified with reference to the existing program, the available resources to support the program, and the competencies of personnel needed to conduct the new program successfully. As we have seen, proposed innovations should enable the organization to be more successful in pursuing its goals. Before it can be determined that they will, an assessment must be made of existing programs, qualifications of staff, and the resources available.

A certain level of dissatisfaction with present programs, in whole or in part, must exist before innovations will be introduced. The percentage of persons in an organization who would have to experience such dissatisfaction is likely to be small, since major innovations originate within the administrative hierarchy, but the success of new programs usually depends on gaining the support of personnel in carrying them out. Hence, skill in human relations looms large here, for support is not likely to be forthcoming unless the sponsors of innovation can convince those who will be responsible for carrying out the new program of the merits of the plan.

One way to create interest in the need for new programs is to arouse dissatisfaction with existing programs. It is not so much that new programs are sought, evaluated, and rejected as that there is little dissatisfaction with present programs and a general resistance to change because of its disruptive effect on routines and established practices. According to March and Simon, in the search for new programs the variables that will be used first are those under organizational control. If this approach should prove inadequte, the organization will direct attention to variables not under direct control. If a satisfactory program is still not found, the original criteria for the program will be reexamined and they will probably be redefined less stringently in order that the program may succeed.* In other words, organizations are limited by the

---

* James G. March and Herbert A. Simon, *Organizations* (New York: John Wiley and Sons, 1958), pp. 179–180.

qualifications of their personnel and the resources available for new programs. When criteria for new programs are unrealistically high, they need to be readjusted; if too low, they need to be raised in order for the new program to create a challenge and offer a reasonable likelihood of success.

New programs are more likely to succeed with some form of central planning than without any. Planning not only will include an assessment of the need for new programs and their likelihood of success, but will anticipate how changes in one area of the organization will affect other areas where changes have not been introduced. An innovation in the college preparatory program at the secondary level will bring about changes in record-keeping, scheduling, evaluation of credits, and relative distribution of students in classes, to name only a few of the affected procedures. Those responsible for planning educational innovations need to anticipate the repercussions they will cause in the various divisions within the organization; and when personnel in these divisions are properly informed and prepared for the changes, there is greater probability that they will be successful.

Another reason for careful plannning relates to the concept of organizational control. Only a certain level of disorganization can be tolerated by organizations before a dangerous level of disruption to vital operations sets in. Adequate planning before introducing innovations should preclude their causing any serious disorganizing effects. The level of tolerance of innovation that organizations can afford depends on the success of planning, the adequacy of resources to support innovations, the qualifications of personnel to carry them out successfully, and the level of stress within the organization.

The last term needs further amplification. Stress is the difference between an individual's present level of achievement and his aspirations. One experiences considerable stress when aspirations are unreasonably high. The result will be either maladjustment or recognition of the difficulty and readjustment of aspirations to a more reasonable level. If aspirations are low and easily attained, a very low level of stress exists. Organizations also experience the same phenomena. Organizational goals must be realistic or stress will be too high or too low. With low organizational stress, goals are easily achieved because they are set unrealistically low. As a consequence, there is both inadequate utilization of resources and a tendency for personnel to become complacent. Unrealistically high goals engender high stress, which leads to frustration and disorganization. If stress is either too high or too low, the time is not right for innovation: with high stress, disorganization would be increased; with low stress, a sense of complacency and satisfaction would be likely to prevent innovations from being successful.

Organizations can recognize the need for innovations in two general ways: they can determine that they are not measuring up to their own standards; and they can compare their rate of growth or improvement wih that of similar organizations and discover their own inadequacy. In the first method, the organization must have a clearly formulated set of standards by which progress can be evaluated, whereas in the second, the organization ranks itself with reference to the success of similar organizations. It can be seen in industry that both methods are used. Each company has its own standards by which it regulates its tasks, and in order to maximize profits, the company must keep pace with or excel its competitors. Each educational system, too, has its own standards by which it regulates its internal operations, and there are also standards—primarily those developed by each state for purposes of accreditation—to which educational systems can be compared. Thus, educational organizations recognize the need for innovation by using these two methods of evaluation.

Sometimes when innovations are introduced, educational practices deviate more sharply than before from existing standards. At that time an assessment of standards is needed—even though some may look upon them as sacrosanct. Standards are evaluated in terms of educational goals, and when standards are in conflict with one another, the conflict can be resolved by determining which set of standards moves the organization closer to its goals. However, goals are not fixed once and for all time. Should an organization attain its goals, it must set up new goals or go out of business. This situation is illustrated by the National Foundation for Infantile Paralysis. When it attained its goals, it changed its name to the National Foundation, established new goals, and set up a new program. Goals are also changed by new demands and expectations placed on organizations. Schools today train young people for specialties that did not exist years ago. It has been characteristic in our history for educational institutions to change their goals to meet new demands of a society in transition.

It should be evident, then, that standards and goals should always be open to evaluation. After the results of innovations have been assessed in general, they can be evaluated with specific reference to standards and goals. If innovations should cause practices to deviate sharply from standards and goals, this fact may suggest that not just innovations, but all aspects of the organization's operations should be evaluated regularly.

Educational Standards

The two general processes found in all organizations are control and innovation; these processes are oriented toward helping organizations achieve their goals. We have seen that controls are needed to maintain coordination within the different divisions of the organization, to provide continuity of programs, and to prevent cases of disorganization from arising. Innovations are needed whenever existing plans and programs prove inadequate in attaining organizational goals. Standards are established to evaluate the many aspects of organizational operations, and such evaluations can serve as a guide in the assessment of the control and innovative aspects of organizational operations.

Whenever standards are used for evaluative purposes, two general processes are grading and ranking.* In grading, one decides if something is good or bad, desirable or undesirable; in ranking, one decides whether something is as good or as bad as another thing, and sometimes whether it is the best or worst of a group.

In grading or ranking, one is classifying educational phenomena according to their worth or value, determined by the degree to which phenomena meet the standards adopted. By making such an evaluation, one has a rational ground for valuing various characteristics and practices in education.

In making an evaluation, one takes a point of view; and with each point of view different standards are used. In evaluating school facilities, for instance, the point of view may be cost, the design's

---

* The discussion that follows is adapted from the author's article: "A Philosophical Analysis of Educational Standards," *Educational Theory*, **17** (April, 1967). With certain modifications, the treatment follows the general approach in Paul W. Taylor's *Normative Discourse* (Englewood Cliffs, N.J.: Prentice-Hall, 1961).

utility for the educational program, the value of the design in terms of the physical capabilities of the student, the aesthetic worth of the design, some combination of these, or others.

Disagreements may arise within a point of view. Two authorities taking, let us say, an economic point of view toward school construction may disagree on the standards used in an evaluation. Clearly, some agreement must be reached on the standards to be used in evaluating from any point of view.

There is also a class of comparison in every evaluation. In evaluating school facilities in terms of costs, the comparison may be with other facilities in the school district, in the county, or in the state. The class of comparison operates the same way with reference to other aspects of education.

The class of comparison varies independently of the point of view, in both gradings and rankings. One can hold to an economic point of view toward school facilities, but the class of comparison may be facilities within a school district, county, state, or nation.

Let us look at certain aspects of the overall process by which standards are used for evaluation. After a set of standards has been adopted, clarification is needed as to how the standards will operate in the process of evaluation. We need to know what sort of evidence will count as meeting a standard. Since standards are seldom completely satisfied in practice, however, it becomes more a matter of degree. As we adopt a point of view and set up a class of comparison, we make a judgment as to the desirable and undesirable characteristics of the practice being evaluated. Such characteristics are usually expressed in terms of degree: "highly desirable," "average," "unacceptable," "poor," and so forth. In ranking practices, we use comparative terms: "more desirable than," "better than," "inferior to," and others.

Standards take either a quantitative or a qualitative form. If they are expressed quantitatively the procedures for measurement are understood, and practices are easier to evaluate. However, there are important standards, or ways of expressing standards, that are difficult to formulate quantitatively. The statement, "The ratio of pupils to teachers and other professional staff members in the high school shall not exceed 27 to 1," is a quantitative standard since it can be measured, provided there is no misunderstanding about the meaning of the terms "pupils," "teachers," and "other professional staff members." On the other hand, the statement, "Provision shall be made for students of different talents, intellectual capacities, and future interests," is a qualitative standard, since ostensibly there are no measurable factors. The latter standard is also at a higher level of generality, since it includes a wider range of educational phenomena. It is possible to transform qualitative standards into quantitative ones, either by using terms that refer to measurable characteristics, or by using a subseries of less general standards that explicate the more general standard in terms of measurable characteristics.

It is not possible to do this with all standards, however, because the final evaluation of an educational system must be qualitative, even though the judgment may be based on a series of evalutions made of less general quantitative standards. That is, one must consider all of the evaluations made on various aspects of an educational system and then make a final evaluation on the quality of the system itself. This can be done by ranking: evaluating the particular system as better or worse than some other system or systems. Or it may be done by grading: evaluating the system internally in terms of the degree to which it meets or fails to meet its own standards.

There are troublesome problems with evaluations, however. The various aspects of educational systems are usually evaluated from several points of view, and with each point of view different standards are used. As noted earlier, school facilities may be evaluated from the point of view of costs, aesthetics, factors of human engineering, and functionality with reference to the curriculum. Even though a school facility receives a low rank or grade according to one point of view, the overall evaluation may be high, because other points of view are given more weight. By the same token, a facility may be favorably ranked or graded on one point of view and, despite unfavorable evaluations from all other points of view, still receive a favorable final evaluation because of the great weight given to that one. This happens frequently when cost of facilities is an especially important factor.

In grading an educational system, one determines the degree to which conditions meet the standards employed and the relative precedence of the standards as determined by the weight given to the point of view. Ranking follows the same process as grading but with comparison added. Each factor being compared is graded, and then a relative rank is determined.

THE ORGANIZATION AND SELF-ACTUALIZING MAN

The Meaning of Work

In a complex, industrialized society, the meaning that people find in work is largely a function of their level of skill and competence and the conditions under which they are employed. Dissatisfaction of workers is not an isolated phenomenon: it is found in all forms of industrial organizations.

Conflict in industry arises from the fact that workers are concerned about their individual needs, whereas the formal organization focuses on attaining its objectives. The problem has always been the discrepancy between the goals of the formal organization and those of the worker, which rarely coincide. It was noted earlier in the discussion on organizational control over internal operations that whenever it is possible to get the worker to identify his needs and goals with those of the organization, the problem of control tends to be minimized. In most attempts to do this, however, management has not been particularly successful. A major reason for failure is that the worker does not find his job meaningful and intrinsically worthwhile; to compensate for the deficiency, he usually seeks satisfaction in informal groups and in areas of interest outside his job.

In an effort to counteract this tendency, management has at times instructed its supervisory personnel to adopt a human relations approach, leading to the creation of recreational facilities, "coffee breaks," and opportunities to interact with fellow workers. Although such an approach has produced a more pleasant atmosphere in which to work, it has not brought about an improvement in the actual work task itself.

Informal groups develop more or less spontaneously to fulfill social needs that remain unfulfilled by management practices. Management, fearing that informal groups may divert or subvert operations within the organization, may apply pressure to keep the groups under administrative control. However, the informal groups strengthen themselves to resist the pressure, and if more pressure is then applied, they tend to become even stronger as the process repeats itself.

When informal groups become useful and beneficial, employees want to formalize them; this gives rise to trade unionism. Ironically, however, trade unions, which are developed to fulfill needs that are inadequately satisfied within the formal organization, use organizational principles just as management does. And as a union becomes more complex, it assumes the characteristics of a bureaucracy—some of the very characteristics that alienated the worker in the first place. Thus, the bureaucratic structure of trade unions gives rise to the same problem found in industrial organizations: lack of interest, apathy, dependency, and submissiveness.

Informal groups develop norms that regulate employees' behavior in relation to management. Norms regulate the amount of work that should be done in work groups and govern the relationship between employees and supervisors. Workers are cautioned against turning out more work than the group average ("rate-buster"), and against producing too little work ("chiseler"). No worker should tell a supervisor anything derogatory about a fellow worker ("squealer"). And informal group norms expect supervisors not to act as though they consider themselves better than the workers. Thus, the informal group norms regulate behavior with reference to associates and supervisors, and they also determine the amount of work that will be produced. Informal groups can place considerable pressure on workers to comply with the norms, and such groups have the power to ostracize and isolate violators. It is usually the informal group (rather than management) that determines the output of work, even though management may try to upset this arrangement by using incentives and a human relations approach.

We have seen that the establishment of informal groups and trade unions are measures designed to attack job dissatisfaction. Other means are also used: employees may want more money and material rewards; they may attempt to leave an undesirable situation by climbing the organizational ladder; they may accept dissatisfaction as inevitable by becoming resigned and apathetic; or they may leave the organization altogether and search for satisfaction elsewhere. Management may try to deal with dissatisfaction by material rewards, fringe benefits, and human relations techniques. It may also restructure leadership and control aspects of management and enlarge the job responsibility of workers, with the intention of encouraging greater participation by employees in decision-making about work tasks. Perhaps some of these measures will ameliorate working conditions and improve the health of both industry and its workers; otherwise Argyris' foreboding may come to pass that "*we are entering an era where the employee will be paid for his* dissatisfaction *on the job and where he will have his tendencies to become more materialistic and less human (unknowingly) reinforced by management's action.*" *

The Professional and Opportunities for Growth

The dissatisfaction experienced by workers in industry may not apply in the same way to professionals. Since professionals have spent many years in higher education and advanced studies to develop their highly specialized competencies, and since in a number of cases they have freely chosen their careers as the best means to express and fulfill their abilities, their attitudes toward their work are likely to differ considerably from those of workers in industry.

We have noted previously that those who pursue careers in education range from semiprofessionals to professionals. Flexner provides six criteria of a profession: first, it is essentially intellectual, with the tools and manual labor that may be employed incidental to the use of intelligence; second, it requires considerable learning; third, it is essentially practical rather than theoretical and serves some concrete purpose in society; fourth, it has a body of knowledge and well-established techniques that can be communicated; fifth, it has a high degree of organization; finally, it is concerned with the welfare of society.† Lieberman would add to these criteria that the profession grants a broad range of autonomy to both the individual practitioner and the occupational group as a whole; that the profession controls standards of entrance and exclusion; and that the profession has a code of ethics which has been clarified and interpreted at ambiguous and doubtful points by concrete cases.‡

Since the criteria for a profession represent the ideal, the professions of medicine, law, engineering, and teaching will differ

---

* Chris Argyris, *Personality and Organization* (New York: Harper and Brothers, 1957), pp. 110–111.

† Abraham Flexner, "Is Social Work a Profession?" *School and Society*, June 26, 1915, p. 904.

‡ Myron Lieberman, *Education as a Profession* (Englewood Cliffs, N.J.: Prentice-Hall, 1956), pp. 2–6.

in the degree to which they fulfill the criteria, but none will fulfill them perfectly. It could be said, then, that those engaged in various types of educational work from the kindergarten through the graduate school range from the semiprofessional to the professional category.

The professional, because of his greater competency and devotion to work, is usually entrusted with greater responsibility and a larger share in decision-making; however, there are considerable variations among educators arising from an unusual number of diverse factors. Some of these are the kind of employment, public or private; the mode of payment, fees or salary; the level of maturity of the students taught; and other factors. Many who aspire to professional positions are attracted not only by prestige and material gain, but also by the promise of satisfaction derived from using distinctive abilities, as well as by the desire to make a contribution to society.

If one cannot find satisfaction and fulfillment in his work, he will seek them elsewhere. (We have already seen this pattern with industrial workers). Just how important are satisfaction and fulfillment? Opinions vary, but most observers believe it to be of considerable importance. Maslow notes that for self-actualizing persons, work becomes part of the self, part of one's definition of himself. Maslow believes that the path to human happiness is a commitment to an important job and worthwhile work.* Fromm takes a similar position when he states that the basic satisfactions of life are love and productive work.† The question that comes to mind is "To what extent can people in our society find genuine satisfaction in their work?" From our survey so far, it does not appear that many people are finding such satisfactions. Friedman and Havighurst, in a study of steel workers, miners, sales persons, skilled workers, and doctors, found that workers of lower skill and at lower socio-economic levels more frequently think of their work as merely a way to earn a living and find less meaning, other than financial, in their work than do workers of high skill and

---

* Abraham H. Maslow, *Eupsychian Management* (Homewood, Ill.: Richard D. Irwin, and the Dorsey Press, 1965).

† Erich Fromm, *Man for Himself* (New York: Rinehart and Company, 1947).

socio-economic levels.* What place do material rewards and good working conditions fill in the job attitudes of professionals and semiprofessionals? Does the work itself take on more importance and have greater significance in their lives than do any other factors?

An interview study that asked accountants and engineers in industry to relate past situations in which they felt especially good or bad about their jobs, revealed certain factors that influenced short- and long-range attitudes.† Factors associated with long-term changes in job attitudes were found to be work itself, responsibility, and advancement, whereas those of the short-term variety were more likely to be achievement or recognition. The long-term changes in job attitudes were more singularly potent. The factors found to influence work can be classified as those of the job itself (motivating factors) and those surrounding the job context (hygiene factors). Motivating factors enable the individual to attain his aspirations; hygiene factors help him to avoid unpleasant situations. Motivating factors are of the short- and long-term variety that influence job attitudes. The hygiene factors consist of fair treatment in working conditions, supervision, compensation, and administrative practices; however their fulfillment does not lead to high levels of job performance. Salary, a factor in hygiene, does not lead to high levels of job satisfaction, but only contributes to the avoidance of dissatisfaction.

It must be remembered that the study was made of industrial accountants (who probably could be classified as semiprofessionals) and engineers (most likely classified as professionals); the findings would not apply to assembly line workers and others of similar occupation, who, because of inherent dissatisfaction with their jobs, rely on external or hygiene factors for some measure of satisfaction. For educators motivational factors as well as those of hygiene are probably operative, since it is unlikely that educators could continue to develop and improve their professional competencies and gain genuine satisfaction from the utilization of their skills

---

* Eugene Friedman and Robert J. Havighurst, *The Meaning of Work and Retirement* (Chicago: University of Chicago Press, 1954).

† Frederick Herzberg, Bernard Mausner, and Barbara Block Snyderman, *The Motivation to Work* (New York: John Wiley and Sons, 1959).

without such motivating factors. The hygiene factors are necessary for a work environment free from annoyances, dissatisfactions, and impediments to productive work.

Whenever we have professional people with good psychological health who can find in their work creative opportunities for personal expression, achievement, and advancement, and whenever we have educational leaders who themselves are self-actualizing persons and who take pleasure in the growth of other people, then good educational systems will be the result. The great need today extends beyond the school systems and the teacher education programs that supply their staffs to the image of teaching itself. The problem is one of attracting a larger proportion of outstanding young people into educational careers.

FOR FURTHER READING

Argyris, Chris. *Personality and Organization.* New York: Harper and Brothers, 1957.

Barnard, C. I. *The Functions of the Executive.* Cambridge: Harvard University Press, 1940.

Barton, Allen H. *Organizational Measurement.* New York: College Entrance Examination Board, 1961.

Blau, Peter M., and W. Richard Scott. *Formal Organizations.* San Francisco: Chandler, 1962.

Callahan, Raymond E. *Education and the Cult of Efficiency.* Chicago: University of Chicago Press, 1962.

Clark, Burton R. *Educating the Expert Society.* San Francisco: Chandler, 1962.

Corwin, Ronald G. *A Sociology of Education.* New York: Appleton-Century-Crofts, 1965.

Etzioni, Amitai (ed.). *Complex Organizations: A Sociological Reader.* New York: Holt, Rinehart and Winston, 1961.

Herzberg, Frederick, Bernard Mausner, and Barbara Block Snyderman. *The Motivation to Work.* New York: John Wiley and Sons, 1959.

Homans, George C. *The Human Group.* New York: Harcourt, Brace, 1950.

March, James G. (ed.). *Handbook of Organizations.* Chicago: Rand McNally, 1966.

March, James G., and Herbert A. Simon. *Organizations.* New York: John Wiley and Sons, 1958.

Maslow, Abraham H. *Eupsychian Management.* Homewood, Ill.: Richard D. Irwin, 1965.

Merton, Robert K. *Social Theory and Social Structure* (Rev. ed.). New York: Free Press, 1957.

Peabody, Robert L. *Organizational Authority.* New York: Atherton Press, 1964.

Presthus, Robert. *The Organizational Society.* New York: Alfred A. Knopf, 1962. (Vintage Edition also available.)

Roethlisberger, F. J., and W. J. Dickson. *Management and the Worker.* Cambridge: Harvard University Press, 1941.

Weber, Max. *The Theory of Social and Economic Organization.* Translated by A. M. Henderson and Talcott Parsons. New York: Free Press, 1957.

CHAPTER THREE

MORAL VALUES AND EDUCATION

THE MORALLY AUTONOMOUS INDIVIDUAL

We shall now consider some of the major problems of developing the morally autonomous individual. Several factors associated with the moral life, such as conscience, authority, and commitment are examined; then, in turn, the problems of justifying the moral life and teaching moral judgments are analyzed; finally, the chapter closes with a study of moral development in youth and then relates previous problems to moral autonomy and self-actualization.

The theme of the present chapter is that the aim of moral education is to develop the morally autonomous individual. To determine the characteristics of the morally autonomous person, we may first examine several different interpretations found in the literature. Later, alternatives, which differ from that of moral autonomy, will be evaluated.

A number of studies have shown that among the major problems of our time are the rise of a "herd" consciousness, loss of identity, dehumanization, exploitation of others, "other-directedness," insecurity and defensiveness, and lack of direction and meaning in life. In various and diverse forms the theme has been reiterated that contemporary man derives his values from the group, that he has few independent beliefs or convictions, and that the average or "normal" person has little idea of who he is or where he is going.* These tendencies, which allegedly are widely prevalent in our culture, militate against the development of moral autonomy. Furthermore, it can be argued that moral autonomy is not the expected pattern of development in our society; instead, conformism and adjustment are more dominant modes of life. However, there is still sufficient openness in some segments of our society to tolerate —if not to approve—those who wish to move in the direction of greater autonomy.

But let us look now at some of the characteristics of the morally autonomous individual in order to gain a clearer conception of the problems that such an individual faces in contemporary society. One of the chief characteristics of moral autonomy lies in the basis for individual evaluation of life. In speaking of the individual who has undergone successful counseling, Carl Rogers notes:

The individual increasingly comes to feel that the locus of evaluation lies within himself. Less and less does he look to others for approval or disapproval; for standards to live by; for decisions and choices. He recognizes that it rests within himself to choose; that the only question that matters is: "Am I living in a way that is deeply satisfying to me, and which truly expresses me?" This I think is the most important question for the creative individual.†

This characteristic is further illustrated by Maslow's self-actualizing persons who are ruled by their own characters more than by the rules of society.‡ Since the self-actualizing have in the past had enough fulfillment of the needs of safety, respect, love, and belongingness, they can concentrate on their growth and the development of their own potentialities, and they are less dependent on extrinsic satisfactions and on other people. In fact, they may

---

* For examples of the studies, see: Erich Fromm, *Escape from Freedom* (New York: Farrar and Rinehart, 1941); D. Riesman, N. Glazer, and R. Denney, *The Lonely Crowd* (New Haven: Yale University Press, 1950); William H. Whyte, Jr., *The Organization Man* (New York: Simon and Schuster, 1956).

† Carl R. Rogers, *On Becoming a Person* (Boston: Houghton Mifflin, 1961), p. 119.

‡ A. H. Maslow, *Motivation and Personality* (New York: Harper and Brothers, 1954).

be hampered by others. The determinants of the good life for them are derived from within themselves rather than from social contact.

Perhaps a note of alarm should be sounded at this point: to encourage persons to act in this manner would not only be irresponsible; it might indeed lead to anarchy. The individual as a citizen is obligated to obey the laws of the land and comply with the dictates of society. If each individual were free to decide in each case which laws he wishes to obey and which social conventions he wishes to observe, society would soon collapse. The individual is not a law unto himself; to hold that he is would lead to widespread irresponsibility.

There is an assumption in the above position that needs to be clarified. It is that laws, conventions, and group standards are a higher form of morality that must take precedence over the individual's independently derived standard of morality. However, the place of dissent in American life is constitutionally guaranteed, and disagreement in our society centers primarily on means and application rather than substance. Those who disagree with certain practices are not rejecting the basis upon which society is constructed (as does the revolutionary), but are dissenting from a law or series of laws; norms, conventions, or practices.* The real issue here is not whether the individual should move morally to the point where the locus of evaluation lies within himself (for he would be relinquishing an essential part of his humanness if he did not). Rather it is the extent of the individual's responsibility toward society as he formulates and puts into practice his own value system.

In examining other positions, we find that *"the good for the existentialist is always a positive affirmation of the self. Evil lies in following the crowd. However, the free choice of an act involves a personal responsibility for its commission."* † The assumption of personal responsibility is the very thing that we find modern man failing to do, for in his slavish dependence on the good opinion

---

* For further discussion, see John Martin Rich, "Civil Disobedience and Teacher Strikes," *Phi Delta Kappan*, 45 (December, 1963), pp. 151–154.

† George F. Kneller, *Existentialism and Education* (New York: John Wiley Science Editions, 1964), p. 65.

of others and his identification and immersion in the group, he has been able to maintain his anonymity—to be only a "face in the crowd," so to speak—and proclaim all decisions that go awry to be group decisions. The taking of responsibility is often a frightening experience; the individual is more likely to want, as Fromm would say, to "escape from freedom." There is a certain dreadfulness in freedom that many cannot face, and they attempt to protect themselves at the personal level by erecting elaborate defense mechanisms and to shield themselves at the social level through the anonymity of the group. We will return to this theme later to see in more detail the tendency of modern man to blame others; we will also look at the allegedly uncontrollable background factors that influence behavior.

So far we have held that the morally autonomous person characteristically finds the locus of evaluation within himself, assumes responsibility for his acts, and is self-governing as he strives for freedom and mastery. We can now join with Angyal and postulate two different but complementary orientations in the individual.* One is that the organism tends to strive for increased autonomy, even though there are heteronomous influences that decrease it. According to this theory, the life process is characterized by two components: autonomy and heteronomy, or self-government and government from outside.

Angyal suggests not only that there can be a lack of autonomy (one of the characteristics of neurotic living) but that there can be an excess of autonomous striving. A lack of autonomy shows itself at the personal level as excessive conformism, inability to form independent judgments or to disagree with anyone, and dependence on others far in excess of objective necessity. Less widely recognized than an absence of autonomy is excessive autonomous striving which is also undesirable. The characteristic behavior pattern includes extreme resentment and rejection of the influence of others, intolerance and rebelliousness, and the need to continually test or "prove" oneself by acts designed to show competence or mastery.† Excessive autonomous striving, frequently

---

* Andras Angyal, *Neurosis and Treatment: A Holistic Approach* (New York: John Wiley and Sons, 1965).

† *Ibid.*, p. 12.

the pattern of adolescents and adults who are unsure of their mastery over their environment, should not be confused with the healthy form of behavior characteristic of the morally autonomous individual.

The second orientation to life, according to Angyal, is that of "homonomy": *"The person behaves as if he were seeking a place for himself in a larger unit of which he strives to become a part."* * One should note, however, that the two orientations in the well-integrated person are complementary rather than conflicting.

As one strives to master and govern the environment, one discovers that one cannot do this effectively by direct application of force, by sheer violence. One must understand and respect the laws of the environment, go along with them, so to say, which means assuming a homonomous attitude. On the other hand, bringing one's best to a loving relationship requires not only a capacity for self-surrender but also a degree of proficient mastery of one's world, of resourcefulness and self-reliance.†

Autonomy and homonomy are apparently complementary orientations that have their norms of healthy expression. On the other hand, Maslow's self-actualizing person, having received enough love, respect, and sense of belonging, seems to operate on the level of homonomy less often than those who are less healthy.

The complementary orientations of autonomy and homonomy can be found in Riesman's interpretation of the autonomous person as one who is capable of conforming to societal norms but free to choose whether or not to conform; he is less the creature of circumstances than other characterological types, such as "tradition-directed," "inner-directed," and "other-directed" persons.‡

Frankena and others hold that to be autonomous the individual must increasingly make firsthand judgments; he is self-governing but makes judgments from the impersonal standpoint wherein judgments are open to independent appraisal by others.§

---

* *Ibid.*, p. 15.

† *Ibid.*, p. 29.

‡ Riesman, Glazer, and Denney, *op. cit.*

§ William K. Frankena, "Toward a Philosophy of Moral Education," *Harvard Educational Review*, **28** (Fall, 1958), pp. 300–313.

The individual needs a social framework in which to develop that is tolerant of individual differences and divergent styles of life. Frequently in society today the healthy individual has to rise above unhealthy social conditions of his culture. Historically, those who live in small towns in America have usually been less ready to accept differences that bear on autonomy than have those in the sophisticated metropolitan areas; the latter, however, may provide less of a base for homonomy. Whenever the environment is excessively restrictive and suppressive of an autonomous orientation, the number of individuals who will develop such an orientation is small. But even under the most radically restrictive conditions, such as those found in a Nazi concentration camp, the individual, although he cannot have autonomy in the sense that we have spoken of it here, can maintain some vestige of dignity by finding a meaning for his suffering and thereby continue to find meaning in life.*

More than others, the autonomous individual is likely to be able to resist social pressures to choose an alternative that he would not select if left to his own devices.† He would find that "the locus of evaluation lies within himself," and be inclined to appraise his actions on the basis of a consistent set of principles that he has developed as a guide to his life's direction. The principles themselves are generated from his philosophy of life. The morally autonomous individual is flexible and capable of reinterpreting principles in the light of conflicting situations, he can envision the social consequences of his acts and modify his behavior accordingly; and he can reconstruct his behavior, because his openness to experience provides him with alternative modes of action. The morally autonomous individual is not closed off from the ideas of others and the diverse moral systems found in the larger society; yet ultimate decisions for actions are his own, and he realizes that it is he and he alone who has to assume responsibility for his actions.

---

* See Viktor Frankl, *Man's Search for Meaning* (New York: Washington Square Press, 1963).

† As an example of such pressures under controlled conditions, see S. E. Asch, *Social Psychology* (Englewood Cliffs, N.J.: Prentice-Hall, 1952).

ALTERNATIVE APPROACHES TO MORALITY

Conscience and Moral Actions

The appeal to conscience in moral decisions has had such a long and hallowed history that it may appear to some a sacrilege to claim that conscience is not the sole voice of morality and the arbiter of the great decisions of our lives. In general conscience stands forth as a high form of moral appeal, a type of appeal that exonerates unpopular acts whenever they are motivated by conscience. It is also believed that conscience is the inner voice of man, a distinctly human characteristic that distinguishes man from animals. Indeed, without conscience man would be little more than a brute.

There are certain shortcomings, however, in attempting to base the moral life on conscience. Certainly not all men within the course of history who claimed to act on the basis of conscience have made wise moral decisions. Some have acted not only unwisely but unethically. Conscience, in other words, is not infallible. The annals of history are filled with examples of appeals to conscience by men of power in order to rationalize unjust acts. Since historical records do not chronicle the lives of the little men of the past, it may be a temptation to assume that abuse of the appeal to conscience is a symptom of the affliction that comes from excessive concentration of power in the hands of a few. But there is evidence in our everyday lives that the little man also appeals to conscience as rationalization for unjust acts. One could of course argue that such examples are not really appeals to conscience, because conscience would lead one to just rather than unjust acts. That argument, however, has led to a shift in definition, since conscience is not usually defined in terms of results but in terms of a method of arriving at moral decisions. The results of the method are not contained in the definition. Definitions provide conventional and stipulated usages of terms; in dealing with definitions we are operating at a linguistic level. Evaluation and assessment of the results of using a method for moral decision-making are based on a determination of the degree to which acts fulfill certain standards.

There are some logical misconceptions about the use of conscience that need to be explored. Nowell-Smith has pointed out that conscience, from a logical point of view, does not tell one what he ought to do.* A decision to do something does not follow logically from a command to do it. The function of conscience is that of *"advising, exhorting, or commanding, not of deciding or choosing."* † The process of deciding and choosing evolves from a reflective assessment of social conditions based on relevant evidence evaluated according to one's system of values.

Furthermore, the belief that acting on one's conscience is a virtue and acting against it is a vice suggests that conscientious action is free action, whereas action based on desire seems to carry the implication that desires have overcome the individual and he cannot do what he believes to be best. But man can choose to do that which is wrong; he is not always overcome by evil because he acts wrongly and does not listen to conscience. Conscience is not a freer form of moral action.‡

Another misconception is that those who appeal to conscience find that they must continue to do so in order to have a good conscience. Now this statement may or may not be true, but it is not a moral point of view. In the words of Viktor Frankl,

Man is never driven to moral behavior; in each instance he decides to behave morally. Man does not do so in order to satisfy a moral drive and to have a good conscience; he does so for the sake of a cause to which he commits himself, or for a person whom he loves, or for the sake of his God. If he actually did it for the sake of having a good conscience, he would be a Pharisee and cease to be a truly moral person.§

Thus Frankl has indicated that moral behavior and doing something for a good conscience are incompatibles; and furthermore, there is no innate drive for moral behavior—it is learned.

On examining Piaget's study, we see that children build up a sense of duty in their relations to the world around them.** Some may

---

* P. H. Nowell-Smith, *Ethics* (Baltimore: Penguin Books, 1954), p. 260.

† *Ibid.*

‡ *Ibid.*, p. 264.

§ Frankl, *op. cit.*, p. 158. Reprinted by permission of the Beacon Press, copyright © 1959, 1962 by Viktor Frankl.

** Jean Piaget, *The Moral Judgment of the Child* (New York: Free Press, 1965).

speak of this sense of duty as conscience, whereas actually the early sense of right and wrong comes from responding to the rules inculcated by adults and older children. In short, an external conventionality is developed—a stage each child must go through before advancing to a higher stage. In order to promote the development of moral autonomy in a young person, one must guide his progress from the stage at which values are externally imposed to that at which he makes more and more of his own value decisions. Otherwise, as he becomes an adult, he will merely substitute for a former obedience to parents and other adults an "other-directedness" in which he anxiously attempts to keep his actions and standards in step with the group, the organization, and authority figures.

One must remember, as Freud pointed out, that a considerable part of behavior, especially in the neurotic person, is based on guilt feelings and hidden fears; conscience itself is not immune to such feelings, and sometimes what one calls conscience may be little more than neurotic guilt. The morally autonomous person, however, is a psychologically healthy person who does not need to depend on the standards of others as a guide for his life. He is free to grow and create and appreciate humane feeling as he chooses his direction and goals on the basis of his own inquiry into himself and his relations with the world.

Morality as Authority

All forms of social organization evidence patterns of authority. We need to consider whether authority is persuasive, participative, and liberating, or whether it is manipulative, arbitrary, and coercive.

Popular conceptions of morality frequently hold that an individual is moral if he follows the various dictates of authority and that authority is a repository of all that has been tried and tested over long periods of time and found desirable. To "fly in the face of authority" is to court disaster, for the backbone of society is the fact that its members follow the principles of authority. Furthermore, to defy authority because one disagrees with it is to encourage anarchy. There are lawful ways to bring about changes, and these ways are embodied in the democratic processes of discussion, representation, and legislation.

There are many sources of authority; among the most common are parents and elders, the law, social conventions, and God. The entire process of socialization for children and youth consists of learning the behavior expected of them and performing accordingly. Expected and prescribed modes of behavior are transmitted by parents, elders, and various other adults—teachers, for example —who hold positions of authority over youth. One of the problems of moral education is to determine how the young, who are dependent on adults and who are lacking in necessary knowledge and desired modes of behavior, can eventually move from dependence to independence and develop into morally autonomous individuals.

This problem will be discussed at greater length later in the chapter. The question to be dealt with now concerns whether or not such behavior on the part of youth can be considered moral behavior. If *"by 'morality' we mean at least the intelligent following of rules the point of which is understood,"* * then, for the most part, the early development of youth produces not moral behavior but the imitation of authority. Only when youth are able to understand the basis for what Piaget calls "the rules of the game," can their behavior be termed genuinely moral.

Sometimes as youth are taught to act in accordance with the laws and with the commands of God, their expected behavior becomes transformed into action based on fear of God and fear of the punishment that violation of the laws would probably entail. In such a situation the prime motive for following God's commands or the laws is fear of the consequences, and that attitude has no moral counterpart. For to act morally is to believe that the action is right and that some reasonable justification can be supplied for it. Furthermore, the action may not always benefit the agent. The rightness of an act and what is to the agent's benefit do not always coincide, unless one supports the concept that an action is right only if it is in one's interest. However, this concept can be considered plausible only by ethical egoism (a position that will be considered later in greater detail). Surely we perform some acts because of their rightness, even though they may cause pain and suffering and not necessarily prove to be a real gain for us.

---

* R. S. Peters, *The Concept of Motivation* (London: Routledge and Kegan Paul, 1958), p. 87.

One who acts from fear of punishment may even claim that he does so because he believes such actions are right. Here, however, "right" has merely been redefined by equating it to that which is socially acceptable. If a law or God's will is true and ought to be obeyed, then surely its alleged rightness was determined in some way, and the individual can also arrive at the same conclusion. In other words, one part of the process of leading the moral life is to develop independent judgments about moral affairs.

If the individual finds, after examining the moral basis and justification of sources of authority—and this is a task that no one can perform for him—that such sources are soundly established, then his acting on them is a moral act. If on the other hand he finds them even partly unsound but follows them anyway, he relinquishes his moral autonomy. In other words, if he retains his moral autonomy, he does not really "follow" authority even when it is sound; he "follows" his own position, which coincides with authority.

One may claim, however, that the individual who disagrees with authority really does not have a choice if the authority has great power. The argument once again suggests that action is based on fear of authority. Still, one may protest that the individual sometimes really has no choice, for to run counter to the will of authority may lead to a prison term. But it is a mistake to believe that there is some logical entailment to accept and abide by authority: one can still choose to go to prison. That few do so does not mean that such a choice does not exist. The more common course of action is to register one's disagreement with authority and then work to bring about changes. Furthermore, it may be held that to go to prison conflicts with higher moral obligations— such as duties to one's family and to one's work—and is therefore overruled by these higher obligations. Provided that this stance is not a rationalization, it may constitute one way in which the individual can yield to authority and not be described as doing so solely out of fear of punishment.

Some claim that moral behavior is that behavior which is in accord with the social dictates of the community, its mores and conventions. From this point of view, the individual cannot be a good member of the community unless he follows its prescribed practices. Since such practices are not incorporated into the legal system, various community pressures are brought to bear on the individual to see that he complies.

But one whose code of conduct is based primarily on what the community expects and who fails to examine the basis and justification of community conventions is not acting morally. By examining such conventions, the individual will be in a better position to justify his acceptance or rejection; he must also be willing to assume responsibility for his decision. Unfortunately, many do not undertake to analyze the groundwork of community conventions. In fact, *"Ordinary ethical behavior of the average person is largely conventional behavior rather than truly ethical behavior."* * It is deleterious for both the individual and society that *"what passes for morals, ethics, and values may be the gratuitous epiphenomena of the pervasive psychopathology of the average."* † Nietzsche goes even further when he charges that the established values of society were invented by the weak to triumph over the strong. Men must turn conventional values upside down to live creatively.‡ Whether or not we agree with Nietzsche, we face the task of distinguishing the spurious from the genuine in moral behavior. And the task of a moral education is to develop reflective ethical behavior and moral autonomy.

Morality as Commitment

One additional point should be raised at this time. Is not genuine moral behavior based on commitment? In fact, is moral behavior possible where there is no commitment? Expressions of this position have taken various forms; one is as follows:

The great thing is to find a passion for something or some person and to be kindled in this way. For this, one needs openness and imagination . . . If we never get some central purposes and loyalties burning within us, we never acquire a real inner morality of our own. Instead our morality, such as it is, is flung together from shreds and patches of what is socially acceptable in our group. Faithfulness to the center of worth is the clue to real morality and without it our behavior is like that of leaves blown about in the wind.§

---

* Maslow, *op. cit.*, p. 210.

† *Ibid.*, p. 231.

‡ *Beyond Good and Evil*, in *The Philosophy of Friedrich Nietzsche* (New York: Modern Library, 1927).

§ Marjorie E. Reeves, "Moral Education in Early Maturity," in *Moral Education in a Changing Society*, ed. W. R. Niblett (London: Faber and Faber, 1963), p. 167.

Sometimes commitment is indeed not chosen by the individual but derived from what is "socially acceptable in our group." It is not uncommon for an individual to fear being committed to a way of life not endorsed by the group. The mere existence of commitment provides no clue as to how it was derived.

Another difficulty with commitment is that it may lead not to "openness and imagination" but to dogmatism, fanaticism, and truculent opposition to all who hold differing positions.* Surely the morally autonomous individual is not without commitments. Since he is pursuing a moral mode of existence, he becomes more genuinely committed to many aspects of life than does one whose basis for action is convention or fear of authority. The determinant factor is the way in which the commitment is held. Is it little more than dogma, a platform for fanaticism and intolerance, or is it a series of reflections, open to reinterpretation and reconstruction? Only a commitment of the latter type is consistent with the development of moral autonomy. We must guard against commitments that are not reflectively developed and not always open to further scrutiny, against those that become inflexible and dogmatic. It is therefore important to know how a commitment was reached and how it is held at present.

JUSTIFICATIONS FOR LEADING THE MORAL LIFE †

One of the customary approaches to the teaching of moral values is to begin with an examination of moral issues that are of immediate concern to students and then to move on to those that are less familiar but of major importance. This approach, though popular, sometimes overlooks what should be a prior consideration, namely, that students may not understand clearly why they should live by a moral code, especially if it impedes "getting ahead." In an age of dishonesty, fraud, and corporate irresponsibility, it may not be clear to a student why he should not "do it to the other fellow before he does it to me." In other words, teachers should not

---

* See Eric Hoffer, *The True Believer* (New York: Harper and Brothers, 1951).

† Adapted from the author's article, "Teaching the Justifications for the Moral Life," *Educational Theory*, **14** (October, 1964), pp. 308–313.

overlook the "lessons" students learn from observing the conduct of adults. To begin the teaching of moral values with specific moral issues implies that the reasons for leading a moral life are obvious to all, whereas, in fact, to assume that this is so would be misleading. It would be better to begin teaching moral values with the more basic question: "Why be moral?" Thus the study of moral values could properly begin with teacher and students engaging in an analysis of the justifications for the moral life. The purpose of the discussion which follows is to explore the question "Why be moral?" by investigating some major proposals and the logic of their justification.

The Moral Life and Self-Interest

One major justification of the moral life is that it is in our own interest. It is popularly held that if we help others, they will help us in return; if we keep our promises, people will respect us, and we will enjoy better social relations.

This popular view is not entirely unrelated to Plato's position. In his *Republic* Plato's characters argue against the position taken by the Sophists, who held that to be just an action had to be advantageous. One did not need to behave morally if doing so did not promote one's interest and not doing so did. The Sophists even claimed that an action thought to be right should not be considered so if it resulted in loss to the agent.

Plato sought to demonstrate that the Sophists were wrong and that right actions do promote one's interest. An act that is thought to be right but that results in a loss to the agent should be considered in terms of its effect on man's soul, for the happiness that the just man possesses is a characteristic of the soul. When the three parts of the soul—reason, spirit, and appetite—play their roles in the total personality, the individual is happy. Thus by acting justly, one will achieve happiness.

The Sophists' contention—that to be right an action must be advantageous—will be examined first. Following the Sophists' line of reasoning leads to the conclusion that advantageousness and nothing else makes an action right. Maintaining this involves the conviction that it is a duty—our only duty—to do whatever is to our advantage. If the weaknesses of the Sophists' position are not already apparent, further analysis shows their argument to be a form of ethical egoism, a theory which holds that one should act in his own interest and for his own advantage. The ethical egoist does not repudiate the practice of helping others so long as he stands to gain from such an act.

Brian Medlin * points out that ethical egoism is an inconsistent theory, because the ethical egoist is likely to impair his own advantage by promulgating his doctrine, which encourages others to act exclusively in their own interest. Surely the ethical egoist who seeks his own advantage, must persuade them to do otherwise. But in order to be an ethical doctrine it must apply to others; thus ethical egoism, when carried out in practice, is reduced to individual egoism, which is not an ethical doctrine at all.

Brandt,† on the other hand, believes that the charge of inconsistent attitudes is more damaging to ethical egoism than is Medlin's argument. Since ethical egoism demands that each person take the course of action which maximizes his own welfare, we must approve of the fact that A concerns himself with his own interests, and that B ignores the interests of A. When A is acting, his are the only interests that count; but when A is the recipient of actions, his interests do not count. Thus when A is acting he can sacrifice B's life in order to save himself a scratch; and B can do the same when he is acting. Ethical egoism is guilty of directing action on the basis of inconsistent attitudes by asking us to be impartial to persons, but only in reference to their own acts. It directs us to have one attitude toward A when in A's presence but not in B's, and another attitude toward A when no longer in A's presence but in B's. Thus the Sophists' position is unsatisfactory.

Let us return to Plato's argument ‡ that the just man is the happy man. In his discussion of the tyrant, Plato offers two reasons why men should be moral: all moral men are happy; immoral men are unhappy. The first contention is patently false: moral men or those

---

* Brian Medlin, "Ultimate Principles and Ethical Egoism," in *Value and Obligation*, ed. Richard Brandt (New York: Harcourt, Brace and World, 1961), pp. 150–157.

† Richard B. Brandt, *Ethical Theory* (Englewood Cliffs, N.J.: Prentice-Hall, 1959), pp. 369–375.

‡ W. T. Stace, a proponent of Plato's doctrine, makes some emendations and provides an extensive argument in its support. See *The Concept of Morals* (New York: Macmillan, 1937), Chaps. 11, 12.

who generally perform right acts are not always happy. Plato's view of the soul notwithstanding, happiness for most people depends, to varying extent, on conditions outside themselves. Even casual observations reveal that the moral person is not always the happy person. Morality is at most a *necessary* condition for happiness and it is that only for some people; it cannot be a sufficient condition.

The second argument—that immoral men are unhappy—is inconclusive at best. If "peace of mind" is a necessary condition for happiness, then, from a psychiatric point of view, some who are immoral lack genuine happiness because they lack peace of mind. Yet others, because they are insensitive, may very well enjoy greater "peace of mind" than does the highly moral person.

Thus, despite its popular appeal, Plato's answer to the question "Why be moral?" is still logically unjustifiable. We are more in agreement with Henry Fielding's remark that

*There are a set of religious, or rather moral writers, who teach that virtue is the certain road to happiness and vice to misery, in this world. A very wholesome and comfortable doctrine, and to which we have but one objection, namely, that it is not true.**

Some Religious Justifications

Let us look at another answer to the question "Why be moral?" There are several arguments commonly classified under the general heading of "divine commands," one of which holds that man will be rewarded if he is moral and punished if he is not. Man's reward, however, will come in the next world; in fact, one of the arguments frequently adduced is that since the just are not rewarded in this world, they will be rewarded in the next. This is clearly a *non sequitur*, for the mere fact that this world is unjust does not prove either that there is another world or that it is just. Moreover, to act morally only out of fear of God's punishment and the desire to gain a reward in the next world is to base morality on self-interest, a position subject to the criticisms previously leveled against ethical egoism.

Another argument holds that *"God made us and all the world. Because of that He has an absolute claim on our obedience. We*

---

* *Tom Jones* (New York: Modern Library, 1927), p. 672.

do not exist in our own right, but only as His creatures, who ought therefore to do and be what He desires." * This argument requires, according to Nowell-Smith, "the premise that a creature ought to obey his creator, which is itself a moral judgment. So that Christian ethics is not founded solely on the doctrine that God created us." † The power to create and the use of that power do not themselves entitle our creator to our obedience. We still find it necessary to establish that the commands of the creator are good.

Patterson Brown ‡ argues against Nowell-Smith's position by holding that the statement "God is good" is true by definition, a truth of language and not an ethical contingency, and that since God is the standard of goodness, the statement "If God commands something, then it ought to be done" is pleonastic.

Ewing, however, rejects this argument when he contends that "If 'right' and 'good' are themselves defined in terms of the commands of God, God cannot command anything because it is good, since this would only mean that He commanded it because He commanded it, and therefore there is no reason whatever for His commands which become purely arbitrary." § Brown, however, attempts to show the fallacy in Ewing's line of reasoning by pointing out that God's will is not capricious, for God is also defined as perfect in knowledge, justice, and love and, thus, He would be anything but arbitrary.**

The problem for Brown and theological writers of similar vein is the acceptability of their definitions. As Frankena pointed out, ". . . one must establish the acceptability of one's definition and one cannot do this simply by deducing it logically from theology." ††

---

* R. C. Mortimer, *Christian Ethics* (London: Hutchinson's University Library, 1950), p. 7.

† Nowell-Smith, *op. cit.*, pp. 37–38.

‡ Patterson Brown, "Religious Morality," *Mind*, **72** (1963), pp. 237–239.

§ A. C. Ewing, *Ethics* (New York: Collier Books edition, 1962), pp. 99–100. Reprinted with permission of The Macmillan Company. Copyright 1953 by A. C. Ewing.

** Brown, *op. cit.*, p. 240.

†† Frankena, "Public Education and the Good Life," *Harvard Educational Review*, **31** (1961), p. 424.

Still, the theologians may maintain that because God is omniscient, He knows all true moral propositions and disbelieves all false ones. Therefore, since God is the standard of goodness and is omniscient, man should obey God's will (assuming, of course, that man can know God's will). If one has proof of God's omniscience, one need not be concerned about establishing that God knows what are true moral propositions. Such proof, in fact, cannot be established since teleological and moral proofs of this type are circular. According to Brandt,

The moral arguments, which explicitly use ethical statements as premises, are obviously circular if one cannot know that an ethical statement is true until one knows there is a God. The same thing is true of the teleological argument. It is essential for the movement of this argument to show that the kind of universe we actually have is one of the few possible types of universe that are worthwhile or valuable; so that if the statement that this universe is worthwhile cannot be known to be true except as we already know that some theological propositions are true, the argument contains a circularity.*

Looking back at the theological belief that God commands acts not arbitrarily but because they are good, we seem to find that, on the contrary, such acts are good whether God commands them or not.† Religion, then, is dependent on ethics, because there is some criterion that God uses to establish acts as good—and presumably a criterion that man could use.

The dependence of religion on ethics can be shown in another way. Frankena maintains that theological statements that we ought to be grateful and worship God because He has been good to us presuppose the ethical proposition that we ought to be grateful to those who have been good to us. Any argument directed toward justifying a moral rule must begin with a basic moral principle. *"It follows that justifying arguments rest ultimately, at least in part, on moral principles which do not depend logically on theological and other premises."* ‡

---

* Richard B. Brandt, *Ethical Theory*, pp. 68–69. © 1959. Reprinted by permission of Prentice-Hall, Inc., Englewood Cliffs, N.J.

† See Plato's *Euthyphro*.

‡ Frankena, *loc. cit.* One implication is that religion is not a necessary condition for the teaching of morality in the public schools.

Brown presents an opposing argument to show that the Christian religion is antecedent to morality, stating

> ... it is supremely good by Christian standards to become a Christian; but one clearly cannot decide to adopt the Christian ethic as a result of feeling morally bound by the Creator's command to do so. For if one feels morally obliged to follow God's commands, then one already holds to Christian morality. The Christian religion cannot be logically posterior to any morality.*

Rather than refuting Frankena's argument, Brown's contention offers motivating reasons for but no logical evidence of the alleged antecedence of Christian religion to morality. Thus it appears that the arguments falling under the classification of "divine commands" fail to offer adequate logical justification for the question "Why be moral?"

The Moral Life and Man's Natural State

We have assumed so far that there is a reason for acting morally, even though traditional reasons have been found unacceptable. Could it be that there is in fact no reason to act morally, or at least that under certain conditions acting morally would be meaningless? Hobbes poses a serious challenge here.

For Hobbes the human condition in a state of nature is a state of war, with all men opposed to one another. All men share a common desire to hurt, but the desire does not proceed from a common cause. And since every man has a right to preserve himself, he must be given the right to achieve this end. In such a state, "right and wrong, justice and injustice, have no place."

As intriguing as Hobbes's theory may be, one must stretch the imagination to conceive such a state of nature. For even in the simplest and most rudimentary forms of human life, social interaction occurs among various individuals over a period of time. Whether we examine contemporary preliterature cultures or speculate on the evidence we have about prehistoric man, we know that individuals have come together to copulate and to fulfill other basic drives. When individuals interact over a period of time in fulfilling their basic drives, they establish group life and some system, a set of rules and sanctions, by means of which such life can be

---

* Brown, loc. cit.

maintained. Amorphous and rudimentary as they may appear from our vantage point, they are rules and sanctions nonetheless.

The existence at any time of the philosophical fiction of a state of nature taxes credulity. It seems more plausible that some form of sustained group relations and consequently some set of rules and sanctions have always existed. Furthermore, no system of rules for group life can be categorically predicated on the self-interest of every member unless the group wishes to precipitate its own demise. Try to imagine a group in which each and every member invariably pursues self-interest over a period of time. Is it possible to imagine any result but the dissolution of the group? Therefore a necessary condition for group survival is that its members defer and sometimes completely desist from acting exclusively on self-interest.

What does it usually mean, then, to ask someone whether he wishes to act morally? He is being asked, among other things, whether he will live by the rules that the questioner considers the moral ones. We must not make the mistake of thinking that if a person chooses not to live morally he renounces all rules. He still chooses to live by rules—rules deemed to lead to immoral acts.*

A Moral Justification

Let us try now to see what sort of defensible answer can be given to the question "Why be moral?" We know that a person sometimes performs an act because he believes it is the right thing to do, and he is in no way convinced that the act will bring fame, fortune, or happiness. We must inevitably ask how belief in the rightness of an act constitutes a motive for action. Must one not also have a desire to act? †

---

* Kurt Baier concurs with Hobbes that there is no reason for acting morally outside society and then uses an illustration to show why one ought to overrule pure self-interest in society by playing by the rules. In the illustration one group plays by the rules and the other group lives by *no* rules whatsoever! See *The Moral Point of View* (Ithaca, N.Y.: Cornell University Press, 1958), p. 314.

† An important review of duty and moral obligation in terms of "externalist" and "internalist" positions has been made by William K. Frankena. See "Obligation and Motivation in Recent Moral Philosophy," in A. I. Melden, *Essays in Moral Philosophy* (Seattle: University of Washington Press, 1958), pp. 40–82.

Even if this oversimplified view is basically correct, we can still argue that some persons have the desire to do the right act, even though no benefit may be derived. In fact, there are some who undertake right acts fully recognizing that they will cause pain and suffering. Not all of our desires are self-centered, and the desire to do right is one that is sometimes dominant.

The question is not "Why should we perform right actions?" and the answer, the tautological "Because they are right." The question is rather "Why should we perform this act rather than other acts?" and the answer is "Because it is the right act." * Therefore, after a person has performed his theoretical task of examining carefully and conscientiously what he ought to do and has determined that an act is right, its very rightness supplies the reason for doing it. The justification for choosing one course of action rather than another is that the act is morally the right thing to do. The rightness of the act provides a *sufficient reason* for its performance and answers our original question, "Why be moral?"

We, of course, cannot know the rightness of an act without considering the individual, the situation, and the conditions surrounding it. At this point then we need to seek a reasoned justification for moral judgments and to try to determine the normative conditions under which an act can justifiably be called "right."

THE TEACHING OF MORAL JUDGMENT

In pursuing the question "How do we decide which acts are right?" we will examine a position that has bulked large in the literature, a position taken by a number of prominent philosophers. It is that the rightness or wrongness of an act is determined by the motives and intentions of the agent. One can assess the rightness of an act by examining a person's intention in performing it. A good intention will probably ensure that the agent will carry out the task which it is his duty to perform. This theory places basic emphasis on attitudes and on how the task is conceived, and since the actual consequences of the act are largely outside the in-

---

* John Hospers, *Human Conduct* (New York: Harcourt, Brace and World, 1961).

dividual's control and do not depend on the will alone, it is only the will alone that can be good in the moral sense.

There are difficulties in determining the meaning of an act and its motive or intent as we look at the problem historically and cross-culturally. An act that is thought to be based on a bad motive, such as infanticide, needs to be examined in the situation and cultural context in which it arises. One cannot evaluate infanticide without knowing whether the infant is considered an inanimate being, a piece of property, an immortal soul doomed to perdition without baptism, or a distinct person. Consequently, the evaluation of the motive for the act has to be made within the context of situational values and meanings; the evaluator may not ascribe evil motives because the act is considered evil in our culture. One cannot evaluate the motives of individuals in past civilizations— slave owners, for example, or usurers—without first knowing the cultural meanings attached to the practices they followed.

If "motive" signifies the emotional state in consciousness at the time of acting, belief that the act was generated on the basis of conscience may encourage one to neglect the consequences and social bearings of his actions. If it is recognized that motive is *"but an abbreviated name for the attitude and predisposition to-wards ends which is [sic] embodied in action, all ground for making a sharp separation between motive and intention—fore-sight of consequences—falls away."* * One envisions results only as one has a desire or motive for action; and "will" is the tendency to foresee consequences and form purposes for action. The distinction between motive for acts and appraisal of consequences of acts has arisen in the process of analyzing moral decisions and select-ing one aspect for emphasis rather than another. Motive empha-sizes the character of the individual and his emotional side, while appraisal of consequences stresses the intellectual side of actions. In reality the two aspects are not separated; they act together in the process of actual decision-making.

An additional shortcoming of intention of action has not yet been mentioned. Nietzsche anticipates the findings of contemporary

---

* John Dewey, *Theory of the Moral Life*, p. 18. Copyright 1908, 1936 by Holt, Rinehart and Winston, Inc. Copyright 1936 by John Dewey and James H. Tufts. Copyright © 1960 by Roberta L. Dewey. Holt, Rine-hart and Winston, Inc., Publishers.

psychoanalysis in his discussion of intention: *"In short, we believe that the intention is only a sign or symptom, which first requires an explanation—a sign, moreover, which has too many interpretations, and consequently hardly any meaning in itself alone."* * Freud carried this idea further by showing that the outward manifestations of our behavior—including our alleged intentions—are symptomatic of psychic problems buried deep in our unconscious. Our outward behavior can at times consist of elaborate defense mechanisms by which we endeavor to protect ourselves from the world, from persons we consider hostile and threatening to our well-being. This form of behavior is a reaction against the repressed experiences of the past that lie in the unconscious. Since the real meaning of intentions have been elaborately hidden and masked by successive psychic layers built up through distortions, it may be necessary to go through a lengthy period of psychoanalysis before such intentions become clear.

Basing moral evaluation on intention and motive without equally considering social effects or moral justification (which will be discussed later) seems to lead only to misconceptions and distortions of ethical considerations. Many factors merit consideration in moral judgments, and examining only one facet as though it were the total process leads to a restricted and distorted view.

Let us turn our attention now to the area of moral judgments and the appraisal of action in order to see, first of all, what the dimensions of this process are. For purposes of analysis, the process can be said to have three dimensions:

1)   the individual act of moral choice,

2)   the situation itself within which the individual acts on the basis of his moral judgment and undergoes the social consequences of his decision,

3)   the process of ethical justification whereby the agent and/or an independent observer evaluates the adequacy of (1) and (2).

We shall examine these in order. As we have seen from earlier discussion, in the situation of choice (1), wherein alternatives are weighed and moral judgments are made, one always has a choice although the actual range of choice may be limited. Even where co-

---

* *Op. cit.*, p. 418.

ercion exists, the individual has a choice whether or not to resist it. An individual with an illness in which there is no hope for recovery may be thought not to have a choice. He does, however. He has a choice of what Frankl calls "attitudinal values," the attitude he will take toward his suffering; if, in fact, the attitude he assumes finds a place for suffering in human existence, life can have meaning for him until the very end.*

One may gain the impression from reading philosophical accounts of moral deliberation that the individual, in order to make wise choices, must go through a lengthy process of weighing and evaluating various courses of action. Only then, we are led to believe, will his decision be a rational one, and choices arrived at by other means may prove unsound and unworthy of the agent.

Yet looking more closely at the process of moral choice, we find that, except in a few instances concerning life's most critical decisions, the ordinary individual does not usually go through this lengthy process described in the literature. On the contrary, many of his choices may seem hasty and impulsive to the outside observer. They may, in fact, seem "irrational," if the observer has overlooked the large repertoire that each individual brings with him to a situation in which he makes moral choices. Each person has incorporated within himself some of the dominant norms of his culture, his social class, and his group; along with these he may have traces of several ideologies and perspectives on life, as well as his own individual goals (even though he may not be able to articulate these factors clearly). Consequently, the individual does not decide *de novo* what alternative to choose in each situation. He relies instead on a considerable body of normative material related in various ways to his value system. Most people operate within the normative framework of community and social group and usually follow the prescribed patterns of behavior that are expected of them. Lengthy deliberations become unnecessary whenever an individual's decision is predefined by the social groups to which he gives his allegiance. Only when he cannot ascertain what the group or the community expect of him is he likely to engage in considerable deliberation. Even here the individual can refer the problem to those in positions of authority

---

* Frankl, *The Doctor and the Soul* (New York: Knopf, 1955).

for enlightenment on a desirable course of action. To do so, however, may be to move away from moral autonomy. If the individual wishes to maintain moral automony, he may seek factual data bearing upon the decision to be made, as well as various moral evaluations from knowledgeable persons, but the final choice must be his own, made after weighing and appraising the evidence. He can of course decide not to weigh the evidence but to act on what he "feels" is right. He can make an existential choice whose correctness can be evaluated later during the process of moral justification.

Whether a moral choice is made after rational deliberation, on impulse, on feeling, or by sensing what is right, still unanswered is the question as to whether the choice was the right one. To determine the rightness of an act by the process of moral justification, we need to look more closely at the process of rational deliberation in moral decisions.

Irrespective of the method of choice, final evaluation of the decision always follows completion of the act. Our real concern is the rightness of the act, which can be evaluated only after the evidence is in and the social consequences of the act can be observed. The choice itself may or may not be by a process of rational deliberation, but the real importance of the act is determined following its completion. As for the use of reason in moral decisions, one may still make the wrong decision or do an unjust act if his reasoning is faulty, if he has not gathered all needed and relevant evidence, or if action is not in accordance with a right decision.

One necessary condition for rational moral decisions is the proper use of facts that bear on the decision. Data that relate to a moral choice must be gathered and interpreted before a final choice can be made. Whenever this function is performed improperly, the decision itself is likely to be faulty. By reasoning with someone as to why he ought to perform an act that he previously has decided not to do, one can proceed by showing him relevant facts in the situation that he has failed to consider. There are also situations involving a conflict of values where a full knowledge of pertinent facts may lead the way to a wiser decision. For example, a student may be caught in the dilemma of deciding whether he should honor his commitment to his parents to finish college before marrying, or honor his commitment to his fiancée to marry before that time. There are both factual and normative considerations to be taken into account in his decisions. He needs to know how much course work he must complete before he is eligible to graduate; what his financial condition will be if he should marry early instead of waiting until after graduation; whether the new responsibilities attendant on early marriage are likely to prevent him from graduating, etc. Of course, he has a number of normative issues to consider, primarily the nature and consequences of his conflicting commitments to his parents and his fiancée. But the point here is that he cannot decide wisely on his normative commitments without carefully considering the relevant facts that bear on his decision.

Our moral choices, then, are not made intelligently just by considering the values involved; one must also gather and appraise the facts that relate to the case. Careful performance of this task will ensure that relevant facts are not overlooked, that they are appraised with due consideration for their importance, and that such appraisals are related clearly to the primary values involved in the decision. Facts always have a bearing on a decision. (We are here assuming that the facts are available or that they can be obtained within a reasonable time without an unusual or excessive expenditure of resources.) In some instances one may have made a tentative choice, only to find that he had overlooked important facts that change his appraisal of the situation. He may then, on the basis of the new data, change his decision.

The gathering of relevant factual data bearing on the situation, although a necessary procedure in arriving at moral judgments, cannot by itself lead to a moral decision. An assessment of the values in a situation is always needed for reaching a decision on a course of action. A customary approach to this problem is to develop a hierarchy of values to which value conflicts can be referred. One method used in the past to accomplish this is to place God and religious values at the top of the hierarchy, values surrounding character traits, such as honesty and benevolence, in an intermediate position, and material values at the bottom of the hierarchy. Thus when there is a conflict between acquiring wealth and pursuing the religious life, one can refer to the hierarchy and decide in favor of the religious life. It seems, then, that moral decisions need not be as complex as they at first appeared.

But the problem with using a hierarchy of values is that it induces a neglect of the concrete situation in which values inhere and decisions are made. If a religious value is in conflict with a material value, such as the need for food, the material value would seem to take precedence in the situation. Things are valued not in the abstract, but in relation to particular situations. Or they are valued by appraising patterns of values in situations, and their meaning and import can be grasped only within the framework of the situation. Each situation has its own intrinsic good, which is irreplaceable and incomparable. The earning of a living, for instance, is more important than religious values if one's family lacks the bare necessities of life. The weight to be ascribed to any values cannot be known apart from the circumstances in which they are found; and although every situation may share certain characteristics with other situations, each has certain features which must be appraised on their own merits. In other words, one can generalize from similar situations in the past so long as one does not permit generalizations to encourage him to overlook the unique characteristics of the situation and the peculiar bearing these characteristics may have on decision-making.

One may complain that doing away with a hierarchy of values will only make moral decisions subjective, based on individual preferences and tastes, but this is a misinterpretation. We have already noted that there are certain generalizable features in all situations (even though some features are indigenous to the situation in which they are found and must be appraised only in context). What is called for is the use of intelligence in moral decisions. However, this is no small request in view of the manner in which decisions have been made in the past. Another factor that eliminates subjectivity is that one's decisions are usually open to the appraisal of others; they are also subject to one's own attempt to justify his decisions after they have been made. The process of justification will be further discussed shortly, but the principal point to be noted here is that our moral choices are customarily open to criticism and appraisal by others.

There is a common misunderstanding that a moral decision is basically a choice between good and bad. If most of our choices were between good and bad, there would be no problem at all; and the great perplexity and distress that sometimes accompanies moral choice would no longer be found. Man is in a situation of choice when he must decide between two or more courses of action that are good, or that have some good features. Should a young man remain at home and help care for his aging parents, or should he pursue a college education to prepare for a career he desires? Should a young lady marry and raise a family, or should she postpone marriage until she completes her education? Should a person choose a career that offers considerable security and material reward, or should he choose a career that promises considerable satisfaction and fulfillment but little security and material reward? All of these are real, live decisions that people are facing everyday. The choice is not between good and evil, but between alternatives that have a number of good qualities. This very feature is what makes moral decisions difficult and often disturbing.

A great many moral decisions of ordinary people are based on the moral codes of society, social class, and group affiliation. Much of the time these codes have been so well internalized that the individual may believe he is acting on his own decision when, in actuality, his structuring and interpreting of the situation has been determined by the codes he has internalized through an earlier process of inculcation. Man does not decide anew and on his own in each moral situation he faces. Some writers, such as the existentialists, would have us believe that man cannot be an authentic person unless he chooses for himself. We could certainly add that all learned codes should be open to scrutiny. Just because an individual has been taught that such codes are right and because he observes others following them, he is not excused from subjecting them to examination.

The individual usually does not examine these learned codes of behavior until he finds himself caught between conflicting codes. The likely response, in the face of anxiety produced by this conflict, is to turn to others, especially to those in positions of authority. This leaves him an "out," or a rationalization, should the choice be a wrong one, for he can always attempt to blame it on those who advised him. This, of course, is an abnegation of moral responsibility. Surely, if time permits, he can investigate the situation and gather diverse opinions; however, the final decision must be his and his alone. He holds full responsibility for the decision and must stand fully by the consequences of his act.

Some may ask, "Is it really necessary for each individual ultimately to choose for himself? Is there not some way in which one's choice can be made with greater certainty?" Moral decisions are complex; they are also our most important decisions. This is not to minimize the role of nonmoral decisions; decisions of utility (choosing a new car, a new suit of clothes, etc.) and aesthetic decisions (evaluating the qualities of a work of art and choosing on the basis of these qualities) remain important. Moral decisions, however, make the greatest difference in our lives and frequently affect such factors as success, happiness, and fulfillment in life. It is only natural, therefore, that we seek greater certainty and assurance in these critical decisions.

We have seen that moral decisions are complex because there is no hierarchy of values or set of principles that will hold in all cases and under all conditions. This does not mean that a set of principles cannot be used, but rather that the principles must be interpreted to determine whether or not they apply to the particular situation. If so, then it must be determined in what way and to what extent they apply, and how they can be used as a guide to action. In other words, the agent, merely by having a set of principles, does not relinquish his responsibility for thinking and evaluating in each situation of moral choice. There are also times when his principles are of no help because they cannot be applied to the situation. If the agent has relied heavily on his principles up to this time, he is likely to experience distress and consternation. He may insist nevertheless that his principles do apply and attempt to demonstrate this by constricting and distorting the situation to fit them or by reinterpreting the principles themselves to fit the situation. Either of these procedures, however, leads to unsound moral choices. Although the individual is relieved of the immediate anxiety of finding an acceptable choice whenever his principles prove inadequate, his anxiety and distress may prove far greater once the consequences of an unsound choice have affected him.

Each person brings something with him to a situation of moral choice: past experience, goals to be achieved, relevant facts, inculcated social values and sets of principles, among others. One usually assesses the nature of the situation and determines whether he will act in accordance with the social values that he has accepted. In the act of appraisal he must marshal relevant facts and determine what difference they would make on decision, and he must determine what principles of action will apply. These operations are assessed in relation to the goals of the individual. The question here is, "Which alternative open to the agent will best help him to achieve his goal(s)?" Those alternatives that thwart goal achievement are not likely to be chosen, but there may be overriding conditions that encourage postponing immediate goal satisfaction in favor of an alternative that is in keeping with a principle or with social expectations, or that will enable the individual eventually to realize some higher goal. The goal itself is a value whose worth and justification can be appraised, not in the abstract, but only in relation to individuals with diverse life styles interacting with others in a particular society and in certain social relations. Because of the many variables involved, it is easy to see why individuals are tempted to ask others to decide for them and then to shift the responsibility for the social consequences to those who did so.

He who seeks certainty in all moral decisions can find it only in a closed, absolutistic system accepted on faith or fear. The price one pays for this "certainty" may be high indeed: closing one's thinking to divergent perspectives and alternative positions and to possible sources of enrichment. Those who ask for certainty want to be safe and secure, to have the direction for their lives given rather than discovered. What they are really seeking are personal or psychological feelings of certainty which will relieve them of a gnawing inner fear, not logical certitude, which flows from the development of warranted grounds for judgment in open-end inquiry.

Returning to a discussion of goals and their role in moral judgment, we note that goals are related to life styles. This fact is not always evident, however, because many persons have not articulated their way of life and would have difficulty explaining precisely what their philosophy of life may be. Philosophy of life may be observed from behavior over a period of time in divergent situations, but this suggestion assumes that behavior is a genuine expression of life goals and not a symptom of desires that have become repressed and distorted by the tendency of individuals to yield and be coerced by the pressures of society. If a way of life can be articulated, one could examine the consistency between the individual's way of life and his goals in moral situations; inconsistencies, therefore, would lead to a thwarting of this way of life. But what about divergent ways of life? Can an unequivocal statement be made at this point as to their respective worth? It should be noted, however, that in societies hospitable to differences, a number of ways of life are acceptable so long as they do not lead to a pattern of law violations. Since one can follow a religious, naturalistic, or humanistic way of life and still live within a legal framework, society can sanction each of these (even though one's neighbor may not).

We are confronted with decisions as to respective ways of life that can be adjudicated, for the notion of consistency between moral judgments and a way of life is an internal, not a comparative, evaluation. Decisions as to the respective merits of divergent ways of life can be adjudicated on the basis of how each contributes to and promotes moral autonomy. There may well be several ways of life that make positive contributions, but they are not likely to be equal, much less identical, in their contribution. Thus they can be evaluated in terms of their respective contributions. Another factor is the demand that any way of life makes on the individual to attain moral autonomy. Those systems which promote moral autonomy in less time, with greater efficiency, and with a higher rate of success are to be preferred.

But whenever we talk about a way of life and its connection with the goals of moral choice, we are dealing with the justification of moral acts rather than methods of deliberation and decision; in other words, one usually finds lengthy evaluations undertaken after the act has been completed and there has been sufficient time for evidence to be gathered. Every attempt to justify a moral decision (in contrast to making moral decisions) purports to be rational, since it consists in giving reasons for or against the performance of an act. We justify a decision or an act by giving reasons for making the decision or performing the act.

A moral decision can be justified from the point of view of the agent or from that of some other observer. The agent may be justifying the decision in his own thinking (for himself), or justifying it for others. When someone else attempts to find a justification for a decision, more objectivity is usually possible; however, the observer must be careful to examine the decision in light of the information and evidence that the agent had at the time he made it (not what the observer has later when the decision is to be justified). Of course, the agent can be criticized if he failed to make use of relevant information that was available at the time of the decision. The decision must also be evaluated in relation to the goals of the agent and the social consequences of choosing one course of action rather than another.

In appraising a moral decision, one needs only to verify factual statements, whereas *"Value judgments, on the other hand, must be not only verified but also validated. It is not enough to show that, if certain criteria are employed, then a thing must be said to have a certain degree of 'goodness'; we must show that these criteria ought to be employed."* *

Value judgments are validated in moral decisions by giving reasons for using one group of values rather than another. It is necessary to demonstrate that the value judgments are relevant to the situation in which they are used by showing that the scope and range of the judgments apply to the situation; that there is no reason for not applying the value judgment in the particular situation; and, finally, that the given value judgments are not in conflict with basic standards or rules used for verification, or, if in conflict, that they take precedence.

Let us review the process of justifying moral judgments that has been presented so far. There are present in the agent's experience a number of values. He chooses one as the basis for action. One asks if his action is consistent with the selected value. An examination is made of the factual evidence bearing on the judgment to see if the agent has collected and interpreted the facts correctly and related them to his value propositions. This process should not be judged in terms of what is known about the situation in retrospect; it should be evaluated in terms of what was available to the agent at the time of the action and how well he handled the factual information bearing on his decision. As previously indicated, another question can be raised as to why the agent used one set of values rather than another. In other words, are these values the appropriate ones? We have discussed ways in which such a validation can be made.

There are times when disputes over moral decisions revolve around factual matters rather than disagreements over values; thus a number of disagreements may be settled by closer attention to

---

* Kurt Baier, *The Moral Point of View* (New York: Random House, 1965), pp. 21–22.

the factual evidence bearing on the decision. At other times disagreements may arise from a lack of clarity in key conceptual terms and their implications for the situation. In justifying a moral decision, one should give attention to factual claims and conceptual terms to resolve disagreements. If such attention has been given and disagreements still persist, one must find out if there is some question about the appropriateness of the moral judgments employed; and this, as we have seen, is a matter of validation. Moreover, it should be noted that, in contrast to rigorous logical reasoning, particularly of a deductive type, two or more moral judgments may be equally plausible in a situation. There is not just one moral decision possible in some complex situations; two or more may be chosen. Several positions may be equally plausible in complex decisions.

Finally, there may be times when fundamental disagreements over the rightness of a moral decision are found at a higher order of much more general and abstract values. The dispute may ultimately lie in a disagreement as to the agent's chosen way of life, from which his value decisions emanate. The observer, who is attempting to see if the action is justified, may subscribe to a different way of life and be unable to see the decision as justifiable because ultimately it conflicts with his own way of life. Since the aim of moral education, according to the position taken here, is to develop the morally autonomous individual, it is not sufficient to evaluate a way of life on the basis of whether it was rationally chosen. A number of ways of life can be rationally chosen, but each may result in a different set of social consequences. One can even make an irrational choice or a nonrational or existential choice and still have a moral way of life. One adjudicates the merits of respective ways of life on the basis of how each contributes to and promotes moral autonomy. Since there may be several that have such results, they can be evaluated, on the one hand, as to the extent and degree to which they attain such results and, on the other hand, as to the demands they make on particular individuals in terms of their potentials and resources for personal development. Moreover, a way of life that does not lead to as high a degree of moral autonomy as does another may nonetheless be more appropriate for a particular individual in the light of his limitations and his potentials and resources for personal development.

That which is appropriate in the teaching of moral values depends on a number of factors; one necessary consideration is the level of moral development in children. Among the studies which have been conducted in this area, those of Jean Piaget, the Swiss psychologist, have received the widest attention.* Piaget holds that morality consists of a set of rules and that all morality is based on the respect that the individual acquires for the rules. Most rules are developed by adults and then transmitted to children. Since Piaget was interested in the child's conception of rules, he looked for a set of rules developed by children that would be amenable to psychological study; he chose the game of marbles. He recorded observations both of the ideas children of different ages form about the character of game rules and of the way they apply the rules. He referred to the former as "consciousness of rules" and to the latter as the "practice of rules."

Several stages were found in the consciousness and practice of the rules. In the earliest stage, which is motor and individual in character, the rules are primarily those that grow out of the child's early neuro-muscular development. Between the ages of two and five, the child imitates the rules of others, but either he plays by himself or he plays with others without trying to win. Thus he imitates rules but practices them in accordance with his own fantasy. Since at this stage the child regards rules as sacred and eternal, any attempted alteration is interpreted as a transgression.

Between the ages of seven and eight, a less egocentric and more socially oriented outlook develops. The child now tries to win, and he also shows concern for the mutual control and unification of rules—although his ideas about them are somewhat vague.

Mastery of the rules proceeds by degrees, and between the ages of 11 and 12, the rules of the game have become fixed, and a high level of agreement on the rules can be found among the players. At this age children take pleasure in discussing rules and the principles on which they are based. They recognize that the rules are formed by mutual consent and that, once agreed to, they should be observed in playing the game; nevertheless, they realize that a majority can agree to change the rules. In other words, at this

---

* Piaget, op. cit.

age children's practices and attitudes toward rules closely resemble those of adults.

What is important for us here, if we take Piaget's findings as a guide to moral education, is the realization that if moral education is to be effective, it needs to consider the child's conception of rule behavior at the various stages of his development. In essence this means that practices likely to prove effective at one stage will not necessarily prove so at another stage. All too often, however, findings such as these are not given sufficient consideration in moral education; therefore much of what adults attempt to teach or inculcate goes for naught. As Turiel has indicated, children are likely to reject moral reasoning below their level and fail to assimilate that which is above their level.*

The conclusion of the Hartshorne and May studies of traditional programs of character education show that such programs have had little effect on moral conduct, as measured by experimental tests of "honesty" (cheating, lying, stealing) and "service" (giving up objects for others' welfare).† The discrepancy between preachments and precepts and the demands that youth face in particular situations was not bridged. Knowing about "the good" was not a sufficient condition for doing "the good." Dewey had even earlier made a critique that such curricula assume a divorce between moral and intellectual education and actual life situations.‡

Character Traits

Some traditional programs of character education were based on the character trait theory, a theory which can be traced as far back as the writings of Aristotle. It holds that one's character consists of a cluster of specific traits. In applying the character trait theory, some schools were even known to have set aside a certain day of the week for the inculcation of a particular trait. In objecting to the theory, Coe pointed out that such traits as bravery, fidelity, and

---

* E. Turiel, *An Experimental Analysis of Developmental Stages in the Child's Moral Judgment.* Unpublished doctoral dissertation, Yale University, 1964.

† H. Hartshorne and M. A. May, *Studies in the Nature of Character*, 3 vols. (New York: Macmillan, 1928–30).

‡ John Dewey, *Moral Principles in Education* (Boston: Houghton Mifflin, 1911).

honesty could be found among robbers as well as among law-abiding citizens.* What is needed instead is the organization of traits and habits around some principle of consistency, and such a principle acquires its meaning with reference to the total organism engaged in purposeful activity within a democratic framework. Furthermore, it is a mistake to assume an "all or none" factor as characteristic of traits: a person is not either honest or dishonest; rather, he is honest in some situations and dishonest in others. Mixed behavior of this kind cannot be explained by the trait theory; it must be examined from the perspective of the total person who is motivated by purposes or goals to be achieved within a situation. His own perceptual categories, constructed from past experiences, provide expectations and values that help him to decide the proper response. In other words, the trait theory makes the error other theories have made: it oversimplifies moral behavior. It should be evident by now that moral behavior cannot be reduced to a formula; it is highly complex behavior because it involves the total organism, thereby setting in motion cognitive, conative, and affective processes.

Habit and Moral Behavior

Recognizing the large role that habit plays in human behavior, many educators have found a place in moral education for the inculcation of desirable habits. Aristotle, in his views on education, emphasized the importance of inculcating proper habits, and Rousseau contended that it would be better for the child to develop no habits at all than to develop undesirable ones.

Contemporary educators have also concerned themselves with this problem. R. S. Peters states it in terms of present-day knowledge of child development.† He recognizes the need to develop rational, intelligent behavior in moral life, but he points out that during the formative years of the child's development he is incapable of this type of behavior. He notes the importance of early learning

---

* G. A. Coe, "Virtue and the Virtues," *Religious Education*, 6 (January, 1912), pp. 485–492. A more extensive criticism can be found in Hugh Hartshorne, *Character in Human Relations* (New York: Scribner's, 1933), Chaps. 9–12.

† Peters, "Reason and Habit: The Paradox of Moral Education," in *Moral Education in a Changing Society*, ed. W. R. Niblett (London: Faber and Faber, 1963), pp. 46–65.

to the child's later development; but since the child is incapable of giving reasons or of understanding rule behavior as adults do, it is necessary to use these early years for the inculcation of right habits. For Peters, the paradox of moral education is that each person *"must enter the palace of reason through the courtyard of habit and tradition."* This raises a question as to whether early habit training will serve to promote or to stultify the desired development of rational behavior in moral affairs?

Perhaps the problem stems from our traditional view of habit. Dewey notes that habit is customarily thought of as blind and impulsive.* He perceived a way out of the morass by considering habit as the basis of all activity; ethical thinking, excited by a conflict between habit and impulse, sets up a problem to be resolved by reflective thinking. Habits, according to Dewey, result from the interaction of the organism and its environment; therefore they are not private possessions of the individual but can be objectively understood. Neither reason nor will can be separated from habit. Intelligence offers the solution to problems, but habits take over and can repeat the solution. However, habits have a further role to play: we "know how by means of our habits." The more numerous our habits, the greater the possibilities for action. We have habits of inquiry through which we meet situations, recognize their novelty, and marshal previous habits to meet them. Thus Dewey shows the connection between impulse, habit, and intelligence as used by the organism in its interaction with the environment.

Consequently, it seems somewhat misleading to make a sharp separation between habit and reason. Even though recognizing that the form that moral instruction takes will vary at different stages in the life of the child, one need not conclude that such instruction is a difference in kind rather degree and emphasis. We cannot assume that at a certain age certain developments will automatically occur, or that only one form of education is appropriate at a certain stage. It should be noted that *"there is no point in the development of a child at which he suddenly passes from the age of irresponsibility to that of responsibility."* †

---

* Dewey, *Human Nature and Conduct* (New York: Henry Holt, 1922).

† Vernon Jones, "Character Development in Children," in *Manual of Child Psychology,* ed. Leonard Carmichael (2nd ed.; New York: John Wiley, 1954), p. 817.

MORAL AUTONOMY AND SELF-ACTUALIZATION

Let us return to the theme of the chapter: the development of the morally autonomous person. We have seen that moral behavior does not consist of a disembodied spirit cogitating on distant and abstract issues; rather, it involves highly complex behavior of the whole organism—the cognitive, conative, and affective domains—as it engages in purposeful interaction with its environment.

A serious problem for moral education was first raised by Plato in his dialogue *Protagoras,* wherein he assumes that if one really knows the good, he will do the good. Knowledge is a form of knowledge-action. The belief that knowledge of the good leads to virtuous conduct was seriously undermined by the Hartshorne and May studies mentioned earlier. It should be emphasized that one cannot do the good without a knowledge of the good; but that knowledge alone does not constitute a sufficient condition for moral behavior.

Some may argue that through the process of socialization the child may be taught to do the good. It is through socialization, according to sociologists, that the young person learns the ways of the culture and its expectations of him, so that he can grow up and take his place in society. The socialization process, as conducted in the public schools, is usually the inculcation of middle-class proprieties and modes of conduct. It is a normative system of rules of conduct which defines one's personal and social behavior. Rewards and sanctions are used to see that students comply with the prescribed behavior.

All persons, irrespective of the culture in which they are born, go through a process of socialization, even though the nature and the content of the process may differ considerably from one culture to another. We cannot dispense with the socialization process, although we may make qualitative changes that keep the process from running counter to the full development of the individual. For it is possible for an individual to be over-socialized: he becomes so concerned with group demands and respectable role playing that his creativity and spontaneity are crushed. Certainly the process of socialization can be achieved without regard for the individual and his dignity as a person. Under such circumstances, socialization becomes inimical to the development of moral autonomy. A sufficient degree of openness is needed in the socialization process to ensure that the very modes of conduct being inculcated are open to examination, criticism, and reevaluation. By this measure not only is the individual in a position to appraise the merits of the prescribed practices, but the process itself is continuously open to reconstruction. Above all, the socialization process must guard against crushing the spontaneity, the curiosity, and the courage to make independent moral decisions that lie within the capacity of youth.

Returning then to the problem of knowing the good and doing the good, let us recapitulate: moral behavior is highly complex behavior that defies reduction to one set of casual factors, and the total organism is involved in the process of making moral decisions. In order to see how to bridge the gap between knowing the good and doing the good, we must examine the area of psychological health.

There are various classifiers that indicate psychological health: psychotic, neurotic, well-adjusted, fully-functioning or self-actualizing. The thesis we will develop is that self-actualizing persons are likely to resolve the duality between knowing the good and doing the good, whereas those whose health is at a lower level will have considerable difficulty in doing so.

According to Angyal, neurotic persons have experienced loss of mastery over their lives and impairment of their capacity for self-determination; they also manifest anxiety, which impairs the capacity for self-surrender and for love.* The typical neurosis seems to be founded on feelings that the individual is worthless, inadequate, and undeserving of love. The neurotic's life lacks satisfaction and productiveness; moreover, his marked inadequacies in the area of interpersonal relations make the task of doing the good (if, indeed, he knows what the good is) exceedingly difficult for him.

The neurotic also experiences difficulty in performing the function of developing moral judgments. The neurotic person may be not just relatively but absolutely inefficient in his perceptions of the world, as compared with the healthy person. The neurotic is both emotionally ill and cognitively wrong. The healthy person perceives

---

* Angyal, "A Theoretical Model for Personality Studies," in *The Self*, ed. Clark E. Moustakas (New York: Harper and Brothers, 1956), p. 50.

reality more accurately and realistically without using personal preconceptions and projections as a basis for organizing his perceptual field.* Therefore, we can say that the neurotic not only finds it exceedingly difficult to follow through from moral judgments to doing the good; he also finds the task of knowing the good more difficult for him because of a distortion of reality.

It is almost a truism that most people do not utilize their full potentials; this is true not only for neurotics, but also for "well-adjusted" people. The concept of adjustment is no longer accepted as a desirable norm by psychologists—at least not by the existential humanistic psychologists. One can adjust to crime or delinquency, to bigotry and injustice, to a corrupt social order, to a group that would deny others their constitutional rights, etc. Furthermore, adjustment smacks too much of the organizational man and the other-directed individual.

The cost of adjustment in today's society usually comes very high, for it frequently means giving up a position of one's deeper self and blotting out inner feelings, both from oneself and from others, for the sake of respectable-role playing. One is no longer natural, spontaneous, and responsive to all his feelings; he loses an inner sense of self-direction and a feeling of autonomy in the frenetic pursuit of group acceptance. There is a pronounced tendency for the male in our society to eschew anything considered feminine and therefore "weak," such as art, music, poetry, and qualities of intuitiveness and tenderness. And the accepted feminine role too often is that of weakness, dependency, and irrationality (at least as seen by some males).

There is much about normality and adjustment that is unacceptable from the standpoint of a healthy personality and its limitations for moral autonomy. As for the former:

There is much about normality, or respectability, which leads inexorably to stress, lowered resistance, sapped ego strength, and physical or mental illness. This means that if we treasure health, we have got to redefine the values by which men live—permit people to be themselves, to satisfy more needs and to acknowledge

---

* See R. E. Money-Kyrle, "Towards a Common Aim—A Psycho-Analytical Contribution to Ethics," *British Journal of Medical Psychology*, **20** (1944), pp. 105–117; Maslow, *op. cit.*

*more self than seems presently to be the case. We even have to inculcate the value of being oneself, over and above our role-responsibilities. We have, in short, to redefine normality.**

The well-adjusted person has considerable difficulty in bridging the gap between knowing the good and doing the good; not an autonomous individual, he is caught up in respectable-role playing. Furthermore, his ability to make independent moral judgments is restricted by his obsequities to group demands and expectations.

Reexamining what it means to be moral, we can see that the so-called moral behavior of the well-adjusted may be nothing more than conventional behavior. Such persons obey the laws and appear to be the bedrock of social respectability, but the locus of their behavior lies in following the group, not in making independent moral judgments and assuming full responsibility for their decisions. They are far from being morally autonomous persons.

Consequently the principal direction of moral education cannot be that of the well-adjusted person; in order to develop moral autonomy, much more is needed.

Maslow found that with self-actualizing people—those who are making full use of their talents, capacities, and potentialities—the age-old dualism between head and heart, reason and impulse break down: *"Their appetites agree with their judgments, and are synergic rather than antagonistic."* † He found that, although some may consider self-actualizing people unethical because they break with convention when the situation calls for doing so, *"they are the most ethical of people"*; their codes of ethics are *"relatively autonomous and individual rather than conventional."* ‡ It has been possible for them to move to this level of self-actualization because they have *"sufficiently gratified their basic needs for safety, belongingness, love, respect and self-esteem so that they are motivated by trends to self-actualization."* §

---

* Sidney M. Jourard, *The Transparent Self* (Princeton, N.J.: D. Van Nostrand, 1964), p. 105.

† Maslow, *op. cit.*, p. 260.

‡ *Ibid.*, pp. 209–210.

§ Maslow, *Toward a Psychology of Being* (Princeton, N.J.: D. Van Nostrand, 1962), p. 23.

Of special concern at this point is the fact that the self-actualizing person enjoys relative moral autonomy and in his behavior has resolved, much more than have most persons, dualities between thought and action, reason and impulse, cognitive and conative domains. He is all of one piece, unified; he is also developing higher levels of moral autonomy. The self-actualizing person has bridged the gap between knowing the good and doing the good. The psychological impediments that restrict the well-adjusted do not impair him. With his high degree of health, his cognitive decisions are able to flow into patterns of behavior. The greatest conditioning factor in carrying out the good is the level of the individual's health; therefore, if we want young people to be able to act on their moral judgments, we must concern ourselves with what the schools can do to promote self-actualization.

Self-Actualization, Moral Autonomy, and Schooling

There are a number of objections that the school cannot perform, or is severely limited in performing, the role of developing self-actualizing, morally autonomous individuals. Some hold that this is not even the function of the school.

The most serious obstacle the school faces is that it is immersed in a relatively sick society, and any programs or provisions made through the formal educational system will largely be negated by society. It is doubtful that a cogent argument could be developed and defended to show that our society promotes the conditions of self-actualization. We have already cited a number of studies that indicate the widespread tendencies toward other-directedness and respectable-role playing and the conditions that militate against self-identity and self-direction. Several alternatives are open: one can leave all to chance and hope that desirable changes will eventually occur; one can act as a revolutionary, believing that the basic institutions are corrupt and beyond restoration, and attempt to overthrow the existing social order; one can work within the democratic processes to bring out needed social reforms; or one can improve individuals in the belief that they in turn will improve society. We have taken the last alternative here, although in Chapter 1, "Cultural Values and Education," the accomplishment of societal changes is espoused. In other words, this work must proceed on a number of fronts and at several different levels. No claim is made that such proposals will usher in a millennium, but it is better to have a positive program than to sanction drift or support institutional conditions that are the nemesis of a fully functioning society.

The influence of experiences in early life on later development has been recognized since the time of Freud. It is sometimes held that the impact of the home is so great in the life of the child that the school is nearly powerless to counteract it. This is the position that Peck and his colleagues take in their study when they conclude that *"a child's character is the direct product, almost a direct reproduction of the way his parents treat him. As they are to him, so he is to all others."* * What the authors have established here is a new "hard" determinism, almost as inexorable as Freud's. They do not completely rule out influences the school can exert, but their study ends on a note of pessimism by concluding that the schools have achieved little success in the past. Another researcher suggests that the conclusions of this study *"must be accepted with caution"* since the correlations *"have not been replicated by a number of other studies using less personal and global methods of measurement of these family variables."* †

We can agree with Peck's findings (supported by Hartshorne and May) that programs of moral education in the past have not given much indication that the schools have achieved success in this area, but we need not draw the conclusion that future prospects are not bright. Nor do we deny the great influence of the family (even though we may question the strength of the causal relationship postulated by the researchers). Values are taught, however, whether the school consciously plans for such teaching or not. Education itself is a value-infused process, in which the teacher makes value decisions on how to relate to students, maintain classroom control, select material, evaluate results, and perform a multitude of other duties. Some values are learned through imitation and teacher influence rather than through the formal teaching act. In short, valuing is continually taking place within education. Therefore, it becomes a matter of whether we wish to plan such processes

---

* Robert F. Peck, *et al., The Psychology of Character Development* (New York: Wiley Science Edition, 1964), p. 178.

† Lawrence Kohlberg, "Development of Moral Character," in *Review of Child Development Research*, Vol. 1, ed. Martin L. Hoffman and Lois Wladis Hoffman (New York: Russell Sage Foundation, 1964), p. 394.

reflectively in terms of desired outcomes or to let them drift, willy-nilly, because success in such undertakings has not been a characteristic feature of past programs. In any case, when schools experiment with new and imaginative programs, we can see how much they can override deleterious home backgrounds.

A more direct argument against self-actualization as a school aim is that it confuses the role of the educator with the role of the physician; the function of the school is to train and instruct, not to help and cure.

The school is not equipped to assume the role of a mental health clinic, although talk about mental health may lead one to believe that the school is expected to assume such a function. In discussions of self-actualization and moral autonomy, there is no implication that the school should be asked to take on the role of treating and curing emotionally disturbed students. At issue instead is whether the school, if it is to provide an atmosphere where moral growth can be nurtured, can afford to ignore such conditions, any more than it could ignore conditions that foster intellectual growth. In fact, the intellectual and moral are integrally related in experience, either from the point of view of Maslow or from that of Dewey. The former maintains that the self-actualizing person is also more intellectually autonomous and perceptive; the latter that the moral and the intellectual are not separate realms but that the method of reflective inquiry is also the method of moral inquiry.

One could grant all of this and still contend that the prospects for moral education to be nurtured through schooling are bleak. How is it possible to promote desired conditions when teachers and administrators are not themselves noted for their self-actualizing qualities? Have not the schools their share of neurotics and well-adjusted time servers? Since an accepting and nurturing atmosphere is of great importance in moral education, how can such an atmosphere be provided?

What type of teacher is needed? In an article reporting the results of a dissertation study, Dandes found that the greater the psychological health of the teacher, the greater the possession of attitudes and values characteristic of effective teaching.* Teacher education

---

* Herbert W. Dandes, "Psychological Health and Teaching Effectiveness," *The Journal of Teacher Education*, **17** (Fall, 1966), pp. 301–306.

programs, however, have primarily emphasized the acquisition of knowledge of one's subject, of the school system, and of teaching methodology. What appears needed is some form of inventory on the prospective teacher's health and self-actualizing tendencies. That more self-actualizing teachers are not in the schools at present is due also to the fact that the merit of having such qualities among teaching personnel has not always been recognized by administrators. The conforming, "well-adjusted" teacher is more pliant and docile and does not disrupt the organizational machinery. Thus circumstances are not altogether favorable for recognizing the worth of teachers with these characteristics and for getting them into the school system; nonetheless, if moral education is to have a "ghost of a chance," we will have to find many more such teachers than we have today.

What can be done toward developing specific programs of moral education? The schools, as has been noted, cannot effect major transformations in the moral development of youth because of the impact of other factors in their lives, as well as the limitations with which schools are faced. But education does have a role to play. It can provide the atmosphere and the conditions within which moral development can be nurtured. And it can begin to staff itself with professionals who have self-actualizing, morally autonomous qualities.

Beyond fostering the right atmosphere and hiring the desired personnel, how can the schools conduct a moral-education program? In view of the failures of the past, what really can be offered? A school can provide an atmosphere of respect for both individual and cultural differences. It should strive to be a center of inquiry where moral conflicts are thoughtfully examined, a place where youth can learn to make intelligent moral judgments. It can also show that the generating force underlying much of its instructional program consists of the great moral issues that shape men and societies. These are the issues, along with others that arise in the lives of students, that are to be examined in all of their ramifications in order that reasoned moral judgments can be made. . Above all, a school can promote the cultivation of a reflective attitude toward moral issues, thereby encouraging the student to develop the necessary ability and motivation to ensure that his life will be characterized by a process of continuous growth in moral decision-making.

Baier, Kurt. *The Moral Point of View*. Ithaca: Cornell University Press, 1958; New York: Random House, 1965.

Bonner, Hubert. *On Being Mindful of Man*. Boston: Houghton Mifflin, 1965.

Brandt, Richard B. *Ethical Theory*. Englewood Cliffs, N.J.: Prentice-Hall, 1959.

Dewey, John. *Democracy and Education*. New York: Macmillan, 1916.

————. *Moral Principles in Education*. Boston: Houghton Mifflin, 1909; New York: Philosophical Library, 1959.

Durkheim, Emile. *Moral Education*. New York: Free Press, 1961.

Frankena, William K. *Ethics*. Englewood Cliffs, N.J.: Prentice-Hall, 1963.

Frankl, Viktor. *Man's Search for Meaning*. Boston: Beacon Press, 1962.

Fromm, Erich. *The Art of Loving*. New York: Harper and Brothers, 1956; Bantam, 1963.

————. *Man for Himself*. New York: Rinehart, 1947.

Hare, R. M. *The Language of Morals*. New York: Oxford University Press, 1962; Galaxy, 1965.

Hartshorne, H., M. A. May, and F. K. Shuttleworth. *Studies in the Organization of Character*. New York: Macmillan, 1930.

Jones, Vernon E. "Character Development in Children," in *Manual of Child Psychology*, Second edition. Edited by Leonard Carmichael. New York: John Wiley and Sons, 1954.

Jourard, Sidney M. *The Transparent Self*. Princeton: D. Van Nostrand, 1964.

Kaufmann, Walter (ed.). *The Portable Nietzsche*. New York: Viking Press, 1954.

Kohlberg, Lawrence. "Development of Moral Character and Moral Ideology," in *Review of Child Development Research*, Vol. I. Edited by Martin L. Hoffman and Lois Wladis Hoffman. New York: Russell Sage Foundation, 1964.

Maslow, Abraham H. *Motivation and Personality*. New York: Harper and Brothers, 1954.

———— (ed.). *New Knowledge in Human Values*. New York: Harper and Brothers, 1959.

————. *Toward A Psychology of Being*. Princeton: D. Van Nostrand, 1962.

Moustakas, Clark E. (ed.). *The Self*. New York: Harper and Brothers, 1956.

Nowell-Smith, P. H. *Ethics*. Baltimore: Penguin Books, 1954.

Peck, Robert F., *et al. The Psychology of Character Development*. New York: John Wiley and Sons, 1960.

Piaget, Jean. *The Moral Judgment of the Child*. New York: Free Press, 1965.

Rogers, Carl. *On Becoming a Person*. Boston: Houghton Mifflin, 1961.

Shaw, Bernard. *Man and Superman*. Baltimore: Penguin Books, 1952.

Taylor, Paul W. *Normative Discourse*. Englewood Cliffs, N.J.: Prentice-Hall, 1961.

Toulmin, Stephen Edelston. *An Examination of the Place of Reason in Ethics*. Cambridge: Cambridge University Press, 1950 (paperback edition, 1960).

CHAPTER FOUR

AESTHETIC VALUES
AND EDUCATION

Introduction

The place of art in the latter half of the twentieth century is not altogether clear. Evaluations by historians of past civilizations usually consider artistic accomplishments as an important sign of the development of the culture. But today, even with the individuals enjoying greater access to and participating in the arts than ever before in history, our own society has habitually given primary importance to utilitarian and material concerns.

There is the view that there is little time for art so long as the work of the world must be done. Man must earn a living and attend to the everyday chores that are necessary to keep his affairs in order; in the meantime, art must wait. In addition, art "bakes no bread," does not help one to get ahead in a highly competitive world. One must attend to "the business of life," we are told, if one aspires to be successful.

There are arguments that have kept art from assuming a more important place in our culture. A common one is that we are embroiled in a race for survival, and the outcome depends on our advancement in weapons technology through the application of research findings in mathematics and the physical sciences. Since survival has a much higher priority than does aesthetic appreciation, survival needs must take precedence over all others.

A number of other arguments are directed from time to time against art, but many are offshoots of the one mentioned above. Rather than answering these arguments at this time, we will explore some perennial questions about art and man's responses to art and then turn our attention to the values of art for the individual and society.

WHAT IS ART?

Considerable confusion has developed in recent times over what can legitimately be called a work of art. Standards of art have differed in varying degrees from one culture to another within past civilizations and from one cultural period to another. The public is swept by confusion over new movements in the arts and the ways in which these movements are to be evaluated in light of earlier accepted standards.

Apart from an examination of particular art works, certain general criteria can be proposed for distinguishing a work of art from other works. A work of art usually has the power to elicit an aesthetic experience in the beholder. The aesthetic experience is not the same as the multitude of daily experiences that merely stimulate the various sense organs and arouse pleasurable emotions. One is constantly bombarded by stimuli which titillate the senses in varying degrees; yet, in many cases, these sensations would not be characterized as aesthetic experiences. Many different kinds of stimuli arouse the emotions, they do not lead necessarily to aesthetic experiences.

An aesthetic experience, although marked by considerable individual variation, usually leads to a heightened sense of perception, an ability to apprehend new meanings or to understand previously held meanings in a new perspective, an elevation of feeling beyond the world of mundane affairs, a purification of emotion, and, at times, a sense of exhilaration and release from the weight of perplexities and problems so pronounced that their previous significance becomes transformed. Art has more external direction, as compared with the internal orientation of hallucinatory drugs. LSD may act as a qualifier of aesthetic experience in that it may heighten sensitivity.

Art is intrinsically worthwhile; it does not need to serve as a means to some further end, although some art does primarily do so. In representational art, for example, may be designed to encourage service to religion, foster piety, promote patriotism, or to serve some other social function. Such art, which may have appeal in a particular time and place, is likely to decline sharply in appreciation with different cultures in later ages.

Since a work of art is its own justification, it needs no justification outside itself; intrinsically worthwhile, it should lead the beholder to an aesthetic experience. Then too, such works are more likely to prove lasting than others which are designed to be useful as a means to some external end.

Art itself is not an object or product but an activity of man. The object created by the artist is a work of art. Art is the creative activity of the artist in the imaginative employment of materials to bring about a new and unique creation. To speak of art is to speak of the activity of the person in creating works of art.

It is commonly said that the study of art is the study of beauty and the objective of the artist is the creation of beauty. One finds beauty of different kinds and degrees in various works of art. Yet there are works of art that are ugly rather than beautiful or that may be characterized by some other adjective that elicits the feeling tone of "ugly." The artist attempts to objectify his feelings, attitudes, and convictions through his work rather than explicitly aiming to create beauty. Many objects that are developed or manufactured with beauty as a primary consideration are not works of art. Since the artist's intention is to objectify his feelings and attitudes by giving them more permanent expression, their final form may exemplify tragedy, hatred, repulsion, belligerence, crushing power, or hostility. That many works of art are beautiful attests more to the feelings and attitudes of the artist in the act of creation than to the idea that a work must possess beauty in order to be considered a work of art.

Whether or not a particular work is considered beautiful, certain cultural conditions are more promotive of creativity than others. For art does not flourish equally in all types of environment. Some artists find that their fecundity is greater under one set of cultural conditions than under another. Furthermore, the role that the artist assumes in his own society may add or detract.

FREEDOM AND THE ARTIST

Even though artists have labored productively under a regime of tyranny, it is usually conceded that great art is most likely to flourish in those cultures where a love of beauty and learning pervades the times. Examples are the Athens of Plato and Pericles and the Italy of Michelangelo and Leonardo. In Athens a man said what he pleased, and the citizenry participated in the arts. Artistic development finds its cultural medium where dissent is encouraged.

Dissent is a *sine qua non* for both the sciences and the arts. Dissent is a mark of freedom, and societies that cultivate dissent grow in a context of tension, with respect for persons and their ideas and works. Both the sciences and the arts have chafed under the yoke of tyranny imposed by many civilizations, and tyrants, hoping to aggrandize their power and maintain maximum control over their subjects, have viewed the man of vision, the man with a creative mind, a threat who must be silenced at all costs.

Science and Art

Science and art seek to find unity in the immense variety and diversity of nature. To unify human experience, to provide it with greater depth, meaning, and substance is the aim of both. But scientific inquiry is not an attempt to copy nature. It strives to produce order and unity from nature, where ostensibly no order or unity exists. In general art does the same, although the realist movement in painting is an exception. The act of discovery in science, like the creative vision in art, is an act of remaking nature by creating order and unity or by constructing laws which explain regularities in nature. Both science and art search for interconnections and unity.

The differences between science and art are many, of course, and they are not limited to subject matter and methods of discovery. The scientist seeks to construct the laws of nature, attempts to bring his thinking into accord with these laws, and strives to direct the course of subsequent inquiries in terms of them. The artist, on the other hand, who is less bound by the nature of things, may transcend his own conceptions and exploit them for their aesthetic effects on his audience if his puropse is to edify and illuminate the responses of others.

Science endeavors to be progressive by operating in terms of the cumulative findings of past researchers. Its tasks are defined by the present state of development in a given field. Whenever scientists are free to inquire and disseminate their findings to the scientific community, the level of scientific knowledge rises, and certain discoveries are virtually inevitable. The history of science provides ample evidence that investigators working independently of one another have made similar discoveries simultaneously.

Creative scientsts rarely achieve enduring fame since their discoveries become outmoded with the advance of knowledge. Artistic achievements, however, do not become obsolete (except perhaps according to the person who believes in some type of evolutionary theory of art). Progress in the arts may be traced within different schools of thought.

Artist and scientist may both enjoy an aesthetic experience, quite apart from the skillful use of artistic technique or the design of scientific experiment. Thus, aesthetic experiences are not limited to the arts but may be found wherever high levels of creativity are exhibited. When the scientist has constructed an elegant hypothesis or theory, when in the process of experimentation he perceives a new discovery, and when through replication of original experimental conditions he can demonstrate a proof for his discovery, he is likely to find himself undergoing an aesthetic experience. That much of what passes for art and science is not of this quality does not in any way negate the reality of such experiences for those who find them in the acts of creation and discovery. Both art and science in their highest reaches are aesthetic and visionary in character.

Disparate as the work of scientists and artists may be and wide as the gulf of understanding between them sometimes becomes, they may yet be able to reactivate the unity they once had by remembering what they have in common. Artists and scientists can mutually respect one another's productivity and acts of creation and discovery, because they share a common goal of alleviating human suffering and bringing about the ennoblement of man.

At times, however, dialogue between the two groups degenerates into acrimonious invective, when cooperation and common objectives are obscured by the miasma of denigrations and incriminating claims hurled at one another.

Scientists have accused some literary artists of being politically wicked, of having brought Auschwitz nearer. Many artists opposed the Industrial Revolution, and even today their successors fail to see that it is science which has power to alleviate suffering by raising the standard of living in the underdeveloped nations of the world. Science can being about higher agricultural productivity, eliminate disease, and help promote literacy and family planning. One's view of the Industrial Revolution may indeed depend on whether one looks from above or below, whether he enjoys material abundance and economic security or is ensnared by poverty, ignorance, and disease.

The literary mind may offer rebuttal by focusing attention on what has been overlooked by those who have succumbed to the materialistic values of Western cultures: the brutalization and alienation of man brought about by the Industrial Revolution. Attention may be cleverly diverted from the egregious injustices of the movement by extolling the virtues of "progress" and a higher standard of living for all men. However, as literary figures are themselves wont to emphasize, a rise in the material standard of living cannot be equated with human well-being. And it is our mechanized civilization itself which has intensified insensitivity and alienation to such an extent that either the negative utopia of Huxley's *Brave New World* will become a living reality or the awesome nuclear weapons that science has developed will usher in Armageddon.* Turbulent periods between scientists and artists, although occasionally resulting in pressures that force the settlement of smoldering issues, are more likely to incite animosities that may rankle for years and occlude further meaningful dialogue. Both the scientist and the artist obscure during such periods of tension and suspicion their common goals of alleviating human suffering and ennobling man. The accomplishment of these goals can scarcely be realized without a rapprochement that will usher in a new era marked by the sympathetic exploration of common problems.

---

* For further discussion of these issues see the following works: David K. Cornelius and Edwin St. Vincent (eds.), *Cultures in Conflict: Perspectives on the Snow-Leavis Controversy* (Chicago: Scott, Foresman, 1964); J. Bronowski, *Science and Human Values* (New York: Harper and Brothers, 1956), Herbert Read, *To Hell with Culture* (New York: Schocken Books, 1964).

In an age that has witnessed an explosion of knowledge and an increasingly complex division of labor based on highly specialized skills, the Renaissance man is no longer a feasible ideal. That the scientist and the artist have difficulty communicating and do not usually share the same interests or even the same attitudes is scarcely surprising. Whether or not such a condition is considered a grave deficiency of contemporary life depends very much on the values and goals of the person making the evaluation. If one believes that the world can get along quite well enough without such communication and understanding, then there is little reason for alarm. On the other hand, if one thinks that difficulty in communication between science and art poses serious problems for the future of mankind, it becomes a problem of highest magnitude and utmost urgency.

The contemporary world cannot return to or resurrect a golden age, whether imaginary or real; the social arrangements and technological conditions of the past can never be reinstated. The cybernated world of today differs from the past in kind, not merely in degree. Man builds his world by his constructions, additions, and modifications of existing conditions. There is no other way except revolution, a method familiar enough in our time, but one which, after gaining initial support by promising to abolish injustice, almost invariably ends by erecting more hideous injustices than those it promised to eradicate.

If we return to our original problem and examine it from the point of view of formal education, we may note that college students are required to accumulate a certain number of credits in the natural sciences, social sciences, and the humanities. There is no assurance that the student will learn to think as a scientist or develop an enduring scientific curiosity; nor can we say with any assurance that he will acquire a lasting appreciation of the arts or that he will live his life on an aesthetic plane. All that can be concluded is that the person has successfully completed the requisite course requirements. Since the freedom to inquire and create is essential for both the scientist and the artist, those who aspire to such careers must be accorded more freedom to make the educational choices which determine their future development. But it has often been argued that college students are not sufficiently mature to make such choices and that until they are, their higher education must be planned for them. Responsibility for educational decisions, however, can never be gained unless some opportunities exist for students to make choices on matters which have a significant bearing on their educational development. Greater maturity arises from greater opportunities to make decisions and to assume full responsibility for them.

Let us recognize that the freedom to inquire and create in the sciences and the arts is a freedom that must be extended to include the continuing self-education of scientist and artist. Some scientists do not like the arts, and some artists do not like the sciences. Many educators cannot accept a brutal fact of life: certain things bore certain people. Ignore it though we may, this obdurate truth persists. Should students be required to swallow their boredom or be deprived of an education?

The communications gap between the scientist and the artist is likely to widen in the future. With the advent of a cybernated age and an incredibly high degree of specialization in the operation of the economy and in the domains of human knowledge on which its operation depends, policy-making in the future will be placed increasingly in the hands of experts. Advancements will more and more be based on merit rather than seniority, family background, and other presently operative factors. These changes will be disruptive not only to entrenched interests, but also to the worker, whose specialized mastery of the new technology may prove inadequate. The knowledge explosion will reach levels undreamed of, and manpower needs of society, along with decreasing opportunities to become broadly educated, will strengthen the cry for intensive specialization.

Yet such a society, even with its multitude of experts, will direly need outstanding generalists who can keep the communications network open and promote a wider understanding of public policy. Such generalists will not be classical scholars; more likely they will be similar to those rare-minded persons in our time who have sought to bring about the unification of all knowledge. Above all, they must be "humanistic generalist," whose very *raison d'être* is the promotion of human good.

The Artist and His Culture

We have previously indicated that the ideal cultural medium for the artist is one in which the love of beauty and learning is widespread, a culture where freedom of dissent is a protected right and respect for persons is the solidifying force that unites man to man.

But we live in a real and imperfect world. Apart from those cultures where tyranny is so complete that artistic expression running counter to official state policies is ruthlessly suppressed, the culture the artist finds himself in may exhibit a curious admixture of freedom and censorship. In such a culture, he is permitted to create freely in those areas which do not impinge on issues of unusual sensitivity. However, if the issues artists may not touch involve human oppression at the hands of the state or any other institution of society, some will feel an obligation to speak out and draw public attention to injustice, even though they may have to pay a penalty for doing so. An artist may not speak out because he fears punishment and notoriety. Yet art cannot be created in fear, and those who tremble in the face of unjust authority will find their creativity diminished.

An artist may recognize, as did Camus, that art alone cannot bring about a renascence of society; yet without art the attempt to create a renascence would be without form.* The role of the artist is a precarious one. He is caught up in the tensions of the world and in the political issues of his time; yet he must maintain a certain distance from his own society if he is to preserve his perspective. He cannot be aloof and still be in touch with the issues of his day; on the other hand, if he becomes embroiled in the political process, there is no time for art. The artist must remain acutely aware of the dramas of his time and take a position when he can do so intelligently; at the same time, he must avoid immersion in these affairs in order that he may better consider them and provide them with form and offer society insight.† The artist lives with an uneasy tension: he cannot adapt his art to the standards of the majority in his society, but if he renounces society his art becomes negation. The resolution of such tension is decided for each occasion in terms of the context confronting the artist. For each issue he must decide whether to actively involve himself or

---

* Albert Camus, "The Artist and His Time," *The Myth of Sisyphus and Other Essays*, trans. Justin O'Brien (New York: Vintage Books, 1959).

† Camus, "The Wager of Our Generation," *Resistance, Rebellion, and Death*, trans. Justin O'Brien (New York: Alfred A. Knopf, 1961).

whether to detach himself sufficiently to have the time and the solitude to give form and substance to his thinking. There is no ready formula by which such decisions may be made. But to deplore that this is true is only to underestimate the ability of the artist to find a way to live creatively with the tension.

LEARNING AND AESTHETIC EXPERIENCE

We can classify the objectives of learning into three domains: cognitive, affective, and psychomotor. Studies have been made to establish a taxonomy for the first two domains.* The cognitive domain includes such areas as recalling and remembering, thinking, problem solving, and creating. Instructional objectives for this domain range from simple recall to highly original ways of combining and synthesizing new ideas.

The affective domain, which includes aesthetic experiences, emphasizes feeling tone and emotions. It has a range of instructional objectives from the demonstration of simple awareness of aesthetic functions in their surroundings to the highest level of affective objectives, where students become capable of actiing on the basis of an internally consistent scheme of values and a coherent philosophy of life.

The creation of works of art involves all three domains. Knowledge about art and its history enters into the process. Such knowledge is predominantly cognitive, although the affective domain has a considerable dimension through the artist's feelings, emotions, and appreciation of art. The psychomotor domain is involved in that the artist exercises his skills and techniques to create the work; nonetheless, the other two domains are not absent from the process. Perhaps affectivity is at its highest level in the conception of a new work or a new approach to a work, when the use of techniques and the act of creation are at their height, and in the successful consummation of a work of art.

---

* Benjamin S. Bloom (ed.), *Taxonomy of Educational Objectives: Cognitive Domain* (New York: David McKay, 1956); David R. Krathwohl, Benjamin S. Bloom, and Bertram B. Masia, *Taxonomy of Educational Objectives: Affective Domain* (New York: David McKay, 1964).

Although teachers have usually established affective objectives for classroom learning, frequently they have not directed their teaching toward the attainment of such objectives or devised adequate evaluative instruments to know whether or not the objectives were actually attained. There is no shortage of illustrations of such objectives, however. The affective domain can usually be observed in such statements when they are expressed in terms of promoting interests, appreciation, attitude change, and the formulation of new values.

No clear and sharp separation exists between the affective and cognitive domains, although misconceptions about their separateness sometimes arise from the common practice of distinguishing between the two domains for purposes of analysis. Behavior is composed of what Scheerer calls a "cognitive-emotional-motivational matrix," in which a true separation is not possible.* And perhaps whenever we talk about cognitive behavior, we might find an affective counterpart if we were only to search for it. The problem is that teachers do not usually search for it. Consequently, they overlook many opportunities for affective learning.

The manner in which instruction is conducted in the cognitive dimension will bring about positive and negative feeling tone in the affective dimension. A student may develop negative feelings toward learning and even decide to drop out of school as a result of negative affect that the teacher's mode of instruction engenders. Many students never experience the arousal of excitement in learning, the joy in discovering new ideas, or even the painful jolt that comes with a rigorous reassessment of one's value system. Furthermore, some who have had one or more of these experiences only sporadically and in fleeting episodes may, in retrospect, find them illusory and attributable to a temporary state of euphoria. Little do such persons know that, although the learning process would be hard-pressed to sustain these experiences continuously, they should be the warp and woof of learning.

We need not confine aesthetic experiences to the art class or, as Matthew Arnold stated it, to cultural activities, whose aim is to acquaint us with "the best that has been known and said in the

---

* Martin Scheerer, "Cognitive Theory," in *Handbook of Social Psychology*, Vol. 1 (Cambridge, Mass.: Addison-Wesley, 1954).

world." If we consider art in its widest context, it becomes "the qualitative aspect of all that is made and done and said in a community." *

One way that this wider contextual view may be taken is illustrated in Dewey's philosophy of art.† His contextual perspective on art focuses primarily on the aesthetic experience. Dewey suggests that an understanding of the aesthetic experience underlies the understanding of the nature of experience itself. Rather than consider the aesthetic experience as one type of experience (as most philosophers have done), one should consider all genuine experience as aesthetic. Any experience that is a happy one, that combines memories of the past with anticipations of the future, and that serves as an achievement of the organism in the world, can be considered an aesthetic experience. Such an experience has both unity and integration, and it is aesthetically satisfying. The spectator looking at an art object must be creative and use his imaginative vision. The work of art achieves meaning—comes into existence, so to speak—when the observer engages himself with the art object. The power of art is communication of the particular and the isolated into a relational and unified perspective. Since each artistic medium has its own value, no work of art is inherently superior to another. Its ability to communicate and bring about an aesthetic experience is its most vital quality. The diverse arts have in common the aim of unifying experience through sensory mediums.

Dewey holds that the aesthetic experience is enjoyed by people in a multitude of life's daily activities. The workman interested in and finding satisfaction in doing his job well is experiencing aesthetic enjoyment. We should not think of art exclusively in terms of museums and institutions; we should consider it as part of the meaningful activity of daily life. Too often art has been thought to be only for an elite group—those with a high cultural status. But art has more significance than such an attitude suggests, and the task of the artist is to show the connection of his work to actual processes of living. One effect of art is to place

---

* Herbert Read, *To Hell with Culture* (New York: Schocken Books, 1964), p. 98.

† John Dewey, *Art as Experience* (New York: Minton, Balch, 1935).

the individual and the community in a context of greater unity and order. In his use of the metaphor of an organism, Dewey claims that art has a past and future and that it is energized toward some result. That art organizes energy explains its ability to arouse and to tranquilize.

Dewey's philosophy of art was extended under the rubric "art for everyday living," and its principles were applied to an almost unlimited array of tasks, from cake baking to city planning. Haggerty vigorously opposed the separation of art from life and the view of art as a discipline that can be appreciated only by a select group.* He held that many aspects of everyday life—from the home and its furnishings to industry and commerce—involve aesthetic enjoyment and creative expression. By promoting standards of taste, art contributes to social character, useful social relations, and even the economical use of time, money, and resources. Art, he claimed, is the making of all sorts of things "in the fittest possible way" in order to make life more interesting and more pleasing.

Returning to Dewey's philosophy of art, we note that its greatest strength appears to be its ability to relate art to the most meaningful activities of everyday living and to demonstrate that art can bring about a widening of appreciations and sensibilities in daily experience.

But Dewey's statement that what is given in aesthetic perception is an object interpenetrated with meanings and a sense of tendencies brought to fruition may be open to question. For with objects of pure design, meanings and the sense of tendencies are absent, even though the objects are worthy of contemplation. One may even hold that aesthetic contemplation occurs only when one no longer traces meanings but lets oneself be absorbed as a unit by the aesthetic object.

There is also the charge that the contextualist position leads to a loss of autonomy in art. In addition, it may be argued by those taking an isolationist position toward art that the nonaesthetic factors in experience are not germane to the work of art, whereas the contextualist holds that the severing of these aspects of ex-

---

* Melvin E. Haggerty, *Art a Way of Life* (Minneapolis: University of Minnesota Press, 1935).

perience would lead to an artificial and truncated growth and leave underdeveloped the great potentials of art to expand the range of meaning and appreciation.

Perhaps some autonomy should be relinquished if art is to be limited to selected works in museums and art galleries. The contextualist position, in any case, holds considerable promise for school learning. There have been attempts, for example, to show that what are essentially aesthetic criteria are also criteria of learning, and that learning cannot occur when it fails to meet these criteria.*

The question may be raised as to whether there are persons who are unable to appreciate art and enjoy the aesthetic qualities in experience, persons, for example, whose environment has been exceptionally brutalizing. No doubt there are those of whom this is true, but for a majority who encounter difficulty in enjoying aesthetic experience, the cause is probably not outright insensitivity but indifference. The function of education, then, is to catch people up in the excitement of learning, to transform indifference into intense intellectual curiosity, and to widen the range of appreciation of the qualities of experience.

Aesthetic sensitivity may also be correlated with certain personality traits, such as independence of judgment, tolerance of complexity, and the ability to relax and fall back into ways of thinking associated with childhood.† In many persons these traits are underdeveloped, and since they may be essential to aesthetic sensitivity, the task of education is to find ways to encourage their development. These traits seem to be highly developed in the self-actualizing person, discussed in Chapter 3. It follows that, to have a high level of aesthetic sensitivity, one needs the characteristics of self-actualization.

This is only a hypothesis, however, since there may well be other personality types that can enjoy a high level of aesthetic sensitivity. Yet the peak experiences of self-actualizing persons that Maslow

---

* Donald Arnstine, *Philosophy of Education: Learning and Schooling* (New York: Harper and Row, 1967), Chap. 7.

† Irwin L. Childs and Rosaline S. Schwartz, "Personality and the Appreciation of Art," *Art Education,* **20** (January, 1967), pp. 33–35.

relates * are, in a sense, aesthetic experiences which have been greatly protracted and intensified to a level of ecstatic heights.

In conclusion we can note that when we no longer maintain a separation between the cognitive and affective domains but search for ways in which learning in one area enchances, interacts with, and heightens learning in the other area, schooling will be more exciting and fruitful. In addition, as we adopt a contextual point of view toward aesthetic experiences, we can envision a multiplicity of new ways that the lives of students can be progressively broadened and enriched.

BASES FOR NORMATIVE JUDGMENTS IN ART

The task of making normative judgments based on standards for appraising the relative merits of a work of art is a complex process that is generally considered the domain of critics and art historians. Unless we wish to declare that an object is a work of art only if it evokes an aesthetic experience—and we know that one person may be profoundly moved, another unmoved by the same object—we must formulate certain standards and observe how they may be used. We also know that aesthetic experiences may differ in duration and degree of intensity. Since such experiences are difficult to measure, one cannot make substantive judgments on the value of an art object by assessing qualitative nuances and perceptual differences in experience.

There is not one standard in art—there are many standards. And much depends on both the person who is making the evaluation and the particular standard by which he is appraising the work. Evaluations are made in accordance with standards which inhere in different points of view. A work may be evaluated primarily from economic, political, historcial, and aesthetic points of view.

When a work is evaluated from an economic point of view, its monetary value is of primary interest. Aesthetic concerns are subordinated to economic ones.

---

* A. H. Maslow, *Toward a Psychology of Being* (Princeton: D. Van Nostrand, 1962).

When evaluated from a political point of view, a work is examined for certain nonaesthetic features. For instance, will it arouse feelings of patriotism, loyalty, and love of country? Does it depict a great public figure as having strength, courage, or heroism? These are a few of the qualities desired when art is designed to serve the state. The work is evaluated less for its aesthetic qualities than for its ability to depict certain instrumental qualities, such as pride, courage, or devotion in service of the state.

Evaluation from the historical point of view places the work in a particular period of artistic creation in the past, by means of one of the classificatory schemes that art historians have found useful when studying the accumulated works of past civilizations. Other works of the times and their characteristics provide a genre or a point of distinctiveness. Included in the historical point of view is an interest in works for the biographical information they may reveal about the artist, or for the light they may shed on particular cultural facets of an era.

We are concerned however, with the evaluation of works of art from the aesthetic point of view. In examining this point of view, we find certain principles, useful in appraising, that should be kept distinct and discrete. One can evaluate a work to see if it fulfills the artist's intentions. To do this one must, of course, know exactly what the artist intended and then appraise the finished work to determine whether it fulfills his objectives. Actually one may find that the artist accomplished his objectives and still not judge the work to be of high quality. Even more serious, one may decide that the work is good without knowing why, and merely knowing the artist's intention does not supply the answer.

We may talk about the divergent effects that an art work has on people. It may shock them, uplift them, make them feel queasy, etc. But none of this tells us what makes the work good. The psychological effects observed in people have reference to the work itself; it is still necessary to ascertain the qualities in the work that induce such effects.

People make statements such as "I like that symphony" or "I don't like Pop art." Statements of this type, if made in good faith, are no more than matters of taste and cannot be challenged, for *de gustibus non est disputandum*—there is no disputing about tastes.

However, not all statements about art merely reflect personal tastes; value judgments are frequently made, and they include evaluations from the aesthetic point of view. Whenever a person declares a particular art work to be good and in support of his declaration shows that it meets previously accepted standards, he is making an evaluation from the aesthetic point of view.

Although one may disagree with an evaluation by contending that one work comes closer than another to fully satisfying a particular standard, an overall evaluation of art works is usually based on examination in terms of several standards deemed to be of great importance. Since a single standard is unlikely to prove adequate for a total evaluation of art works, multiple standards are used. They may include symmetry, coherence, unity of form and content, and others.

To evaluate an art work in terms of each of the standards chosen is to compare it, and the class of comparison usually consists of other works within the same historical period or movement. Keeping in mind the class of comparison and the particular standard being used at the time for evaluation, we need to know which attributes or characteristics in the work count toward meeting the particular standard. Since standards are rarely satisfied completely, however, an evaluation is necessarily relative. We use such terms as "excellent," "unacceptable," "poor," etc. A work of art is usually ranked with others in terms of a standard. For example, it may be described as "better than," "inferior to," "more desirable than," or some other comparative in relation to other works of art.

The art work is evaluated in turn by each standard chosen for appraisal, and then a final overall evaluation is made by ranking the art work for each standard used. Each of the separate rankings may place it higher, or lower than, or on or near the same level as one or more other works used as a basis of comparison. Before an overall evaluation of the quality of the work can be made, however, each standard must be weighed. Since an evaluator will usually consider some standards more important than others, he will give what he believes to be an appropriate weight to each standard before making the final evaluation.

By now it is clear that making aesthetic judgments in evaluating works of art is a complex process. There is no widespread agreement on procedures for aesthetic evaluation and the process described above is presented as only one approach to the problem.

Can our aesthetic sensitivity and appreciation be improved by studying art history, taking courses in art appreciation, or listening carefully to the remarks of the critics? If one's objective is to enlarge his range of aesthetic enjoyment, to what extent will a knowledge of forms or a historical understanding of various movements help to achieve such an objective? Will such a knowledge have the contrary effect of directing attention so exclusively to what one has been taught to observe that the very process desensitizes his ability to enjoy aesthetic experiences? It is not possible that the untutored observer, with perceptions unobstructed by lessons on what he should look for in a work of art, is more open to aesthetic experiences?

To be knowledgeable in art history or to make fine discriminations about various art works requires background. However, will a knowledge of history or information about the life of the artist appreciably increase the range and intensity of aesthetic appreciation? Clive Bell, among others, contends that the relationship of one work of art to another is a historical matter that has no bearing on appreciation; and although a knoweldge of the development of painting may prove of historical interest, it has no consequences aesthetically.* Ducasse also argues that if we approach a musical composition with a map of what to look for, we will concentrate on locating in the composition the features on the map.† This procedure distracts and limits aesthetic enjoyment. Ducasse believes that a person can gain greater aesthetic enjoyment by firsthand acquaintance with works of art than by a deluge of explanations and discourse concerning what to look for.

But since one needs a considerable amount of firsthand experience with art works, might not access to criticisms and interpretations facilitate the task of interpretation? Certainly much has been learned about art over the centuries. Would not such knowledge contribute to aesthetic appreciation? However, there is another complication in the fact that the critics themselves do not agree and that there is no set of necessary and sufficient standards by which art works can be uniformly appraised. Some of the conflict revolves

---

* Clive Bell, *Art* (London: Chatto and Windus Ltd., 1928).

† Curt John Ducasse, *The Philosophy of Art* (New York: Dover Publications, 1966).

around the ideas of "appreciation" and "interpretation." Even though necessary and sufficient conditions for establishing standards of interpretation and evaluation cannot be adduced, some standards have certainly been developed and they are not idiosyncratic but enjoy at least some measure of agreement. However, when we turn to the matter of aesthetic appreciation we encounter greater difficulties. How are we to determine that one kind of appreciation or aesthetic experience is better, of higher quality, more desirable than another? Perhaps only through a psychological study based on introspective reports from subjects. But the history of psychology has shown that such a method leaves much to be desired in terms of the reliability of data. Even if reliable data could be gathered, however, there would still be no way to make qualitative distinctions between appreciations—unless we chose to equate qualitative distinctions with the quantity or intensity of such appreciations, a questionable procedure whose results would be misleading. A better method might be to ascertain whether present aesthetic experiences lead to the continued growth of appreciation in the future or whether, instead, they stifle and truncate future development. This will no doubt be difficult to evaluate adequately, but it at least moves away from quantitative methods. In essence, there is little or no basis for the evaluation of the quality of a particular aesthetic experience other than the report of the person undergoing the experience. However, we can observe an individual's ability to enjoy subsequent aesthetic experiences by noting whether his appreciation remains basically the same, expands or diminishes.

It has previously been stated that there are standards of interpretation and evaluation in art criticism. What are the characteristics of these standards and how are they used in the process of interpretation and evaluation? With reference to matters of taste and affective feeling tone, little can be said except that they are primarily subjective and not open to evaluation and interpretation. Yet discourse about art is not limited to reports of tastes and feelings; it includes historical, descriptive, interpretive, and evaluative statements. Through the use of such statements, one can participate in discourse that is not based exclusively on affective states of idiosyncratic nature.

In art, just as in subjects of everyday concern, we make statements about past, present, and future. Statements about the past are historical statements; yet historians are rarely mere chroniclers of the past. Historians almost invariably do more. They usually seek to understand and explain events in terms of causes and consequences, and they search for relationships in sequentially ordered events. The end product of such search and research is primarily interpretive, but descriptive and evaluative functions are also found in histories. We will turn our attention first to descriptive statements and then, in turn, to interpretive and evaluative statements.

Whenever it is said that a passage or paragraph describes something, no activity or action is being imputed to it. Describing is a way of using language. A fact cannot be described; it can only be stated. Description specifies the sort of thing that is being described. The function that description serves is analogous to a picture: it aids recognition. Some descriptions are valued because they are exact and detailed; others—frequently those in art— because they are vivid and colorful. Description and classification are not synonymous; descriptions may be provided even though a classification system has not been developed. To describe is to tell what something is like, to note similarities and differences among things. Before one can classify, a classification scheme must be developed. Classification consists of observing the characteristics of something, comparing them with those found in the classification scheme, and then designating the appropriate category for the thing that is to be classified.

A reference to the process of interpretation in the arts is likely to mean artistic interpretation in performance or adaptation—of a musical score, for example. In discourse about art, however, the act of interpretation is one of explanation. In contrast to the objectives of the logic of science, explanation in art is not prediction. One can explain without predicting. The explanation leaves open a range of possibilities, and which one is actualized can be known only after the fact. We can look at a finished work of art and see why it has certain components and characteristics, but we could not have predicted that it would have them. Furthermore, explanations in art are partial: only some of the factors within the work are taken into account. It would be difficult to conceive of an explanation taking into account the multiplicity of characteristics that enter into a work of art. Similarly, as we have seen, no theory of art gives equal consideration to all its many dimensions. In this sense it, too, is a partial explanation. Explanations are not conclusive; they can show only why the subject being explained is likely to be so. Frequently the attempt is made to explain with reference to a particular theory, whether assumed or made explicit. In this sense, the effectiveness of the explanation lies in its ability to illuminate the theory through the use of interpretations of particular art works.

Making evaluations of art works consists of several processes. One makes value judgments, e.g., "This work is good." One gives reasons for his evaluation, e.g., "The work is good because it exhibits standards X and Y." There is the assumption here that standards have been agreed on for purposes of evaluation. Since it is often difficult to reach agreement on standards to be used in making an evaluation, consensus on evaluation does not frequently occur.

It may seem that before we can make an evaluation we must describe a work of art in a value-neutral way; otherwise, we cannot agree on its characteristics. However, descriptive discourse in art is not value-neutral. The act of describing the characteristics of a work is based on canons or standards by which the description itself can be evaluated as accurate, complete, etc. But we can examine the purpose of the discourse to see whether its overall intent is description or evaluation. Evaluations include descriptive elements, for we must first agree that the work has certain characteristics before we can make value judgments.

Whenever value judgments are made with reference to certain standards, the value judgment must take into consideration a class of comparison. For an Impressionist painting the class of comparison would probably be other paintings of the same period. A painting would not usually be compared with all other paintings. The class of comparison has bearing on the standards adopted. The standards appropriate or germane to one period may not be so for another. Thus, one must have clearly in mind the class of comparison before the choice of standards can be made.

In evaluations of art a ranking process is frequently used. One ranks by deciding whether the work is as good or bad as another, or whether it is the best or worst of a group. We compare them in terms of the extent to which they satisfy the standards adopted. It is possible, however, for a work of art to rank high on one standard and low on another. Since one is unlikely to evaluate a work overall simply by obtaining an average of its scores on the different standards, the standards themselves can be given different weights in the overall evaluation. One must determine the precedence of the different standards, grade each work of art for each standard, and then compare the relative rank of each work with the weighted standard in order to arrive at an overall evaluation.

ART AND EDUCATION

The Role of Art in Education

What is the role of art in our schools? What relationship should it have to the total program? In our secondary schools, art has been largely relegated to a subservient role in the education of youth. Increasingly it has been argued that studies which directly contribute to national defense and survival should receive primary emphasis and support. Art has little place in this rationale, which stresses the sciences and mathematics. It has been held that the secondary school curriculum needs greater depth of subject matter. Conant did not include art among his suggested requirements for high school graduation for all students; neither did he propose that art be included in the recommended program for the academically talented (except in schools that are organized on a seven- or eight-period day).* Because of the influence of the Conant reports, the place and importance of art in the secondary school program suffered a temporary setback.

The elementary schools in general, have given a larger role to art than have the high schools. There art is interrelated with other aspects of the curriculum in order to improve the child's understanding of other studies. Although the progressive movement increased overall acceptance of the importance of art in the school curriculum, that movement exerted its greatest influence on elementary and junior high schools.

The conception of role of art in the school program has varied during the past few decades. Twenty-five years ago art in the educational program was intended to solve art problems in everyday living and to develop taste; beginning about ten years ago

---

* James B. Conant, *The American High School Today* (New York: McGraw-Hill, 1959).

the emphasis changed to the cultivation of creativity; and more recently, art educators have centered their attention on the capacity for aesthetic reponse and appreciation through the use of intelligence and the production of works of art.*

The art programs in our schools have all too frequently been given a second-class role to play in the curriculum. And in spite of the imaginative abilities of a number of art educators, the arts still have not been recognized as the potential means for bringing about a transformation in the total school program. Let us turn our attention at this time to the direction that art can take in our educational programs.

Art and the Curriculum

A subject may be taught as a separate and discrete body of knowledge, with no interconnections with other aspects of the curriculum, or it may be approached in such a way that the interrelationships with other studies are clearly acknowledged. Teachers who can maintain the inner structure and logic of a discipline while, at the same time, relating its concepts to other areas whenever relevant, enable students to place their learning in perspective and gain greater meaning.

We will not attempt to discuss the many ways in which art can be taught, but the student may find instructive an illustration of the way art can be used to enhance the meaning and vividness of content fields and to assist him in the task of conceptualizing. Art can be used not only to reinforce concepts but to cultivate creative intellectual resources that lie beyond the original concepts. It can enrich studies and add to their luster and enjoyment; it can also provide an opportunity for children to express their emotional reactions. The following suggestions illustrate ways this may be done in the primary grades.

As children read about and discuss the classes and characteristics of reptiles in their science studies, their work can be made more vivid through the construction of papier-mâché dinosaurs, lizards, snakes, turtles, tuatara, and crocodilian. In the social studies, chil-

---

* Art Education, 64th Yearbook (Part II) of the National Society for the Study of Education, ed. W. Reid Haste (Chicago: University of Chicago Press, 1965), Chaps. 13, 14.

dren can study the work done by community helpers and take field trips to the bakery, dairy, airport, courthouse, and post office. Back in the classroom they can build a miniature community of pasteboard boxes, papier mâché, and tempera, and they can help to draw maps of the model community. Reading can use art to help children grasp the main theme or interpret it and understand the sequence of a story. For example, the children may be asked to draw pictures to show what occurred in the story and to develop maps to show where the action took place. Opportunities to utilize art may be seen in other studies as well. To aid in the learning of numerical concepts, space may be left on the assignment sheet for pupils to draw and color a specified number of birds, for example. Music contributes, too. A teacher may ask children to draw what a particular musical work makes them think about; or they may be asked to draw to the rhythm of the music. And the art of writing may reinforce lessons in science. Children can be asked to design a real or imaginary machine that combines some of the simple machines they have studied in science, such as the pulley, lever, wheel and axle, the screw, gears, inclined plane, the wedge, and then to describe in writing how the machine will be used.

The uses of art and the ways in which it acquires genuine meaning in the lives of students are manifold. The preceding suggestions explore one general approach to such ends. Art in the hands of a creative teacher can bring about enrichment and greater appreciation of the total curriculum. It can widen the range of human sensibilities so that the experiences of life can be enjoyed from new and fresh perspectives.

Art and Human Sensitivity

The tendency to separate the world of experience into separate realms leads to a widening of the gulf between the sciences and the humanities. It is customary to claim that science is based on the study of empirical phenomena and the search for physical laws through the use of hypothetico-deductive reasoning. Art, on the other hand, is thought to be in the realm of expression and emotion. The goal of science is the discovery of truth, of art, the expression of feeling and idiosyncratic representations.

But surely these two areas of our culture are not so far apart as these statements imply. Dewey has shown that aesthetic experiences are not limited to art classes but may be undergone in many areas of everyday activity. Certainly the discovery of a new relationship among phenomena in the laboratory or the development of an elegant proof in mathematics is likely to constitute an aesthetic experience. Realization of the wonder and awe of nature, as Einstein and other scientists have expresed it, is an aesthetic experience. It can indeed be argued that the moments in which scientists reach the pinnacle of fruitful insight and creativity are aesthetic to the very core.

One does not work in the various disciplines as if he were a disembodied spirit, above the flux and change, cogitating on the nature of things. Not only is the cognitive dimension present in our undertakings; the conative and affective domains are there as well. For purposes of analysis, they can be spoken of and examined as if they were separate and unrelated realms; but in terms of the operations of the human organism, they infuse one another, and each of the others influences the one that may be dominant at a given moment or in a particular situation.

We may agree with Herbert Read that all expression and perception are inherently artistic since their functions tend to seek an aesthetically satisfying form.* According to Read, aesthetic sensibility is not limited to art education but embraces all modes of self-expression. Education fosters the development of a harmonious relationship between the senses and the external world in order that integrated personalities will result. Since education nurtures human growth, and growth is apparent only through expression, education may be defined as the cultivation of the modes of expression. Read concludes, therefore, that education should aim at the creation of artists: a high cultivation in students of the various modes of expression.

All areas of the curriculum may contribute in varying degrees to the development of aesthetic sensibilities and the cultivation of the various modes of expression. For these goals to become reality, however, considerable attention must be given to the organization of existing programs and the manner in which they are now taught. Furthermore, even restructuring the programs will

---

* Herbert Read, *Education Through Art* (London: Faber and Faber, 1943).

not guarantee attainment of the goal. Teachers will need to relate themselves more imaginatively and creatively to their students than they do in some schools today.

A current problem arises from the belief that the search for truth must be an impersonal and disinterested pursuit in which human feelings have no place. Acting on this belief leads to the dissociation of feelings from actions, a blunting of sensibilities, and a repudiation of inner emotions and strivings. We would reach a more satisfactory solution by encouraging sensibilities along with intellectual capacities to work together in furnishing more humane directions for individual and social undertakings. If we were less ready to discourage children from relating feelings to action, we might succeed in reducing the seemingly insuperable tasks confronting our schools in fostering expression in older youth.

AESTHETICS AND MORAL VALUES

Philosophers in the past separated aesthetic and moral judgments. They contended that aesthetic judgments are focused on appreciation and not intended to lead to practical activity, whereas moral judgments are directed toward getting people to act in certain desirable ways. Such sharp distinction becomes untenable, however, when we consider that aesthetic judgments about a work in progress may direct the artist's future behavior as he works with his medium. Furthermore, aesthetic judgments may also be instrumental in guiding the activities and perceptions of observers of art. On the other hand, moral judgments may indeed be appreciative and not intended primarily to direct conduct. One may say, for example, "I liked the way you intervened to keep the combatants apart and settle the dispute amicably."

The alleged separation between the two realms of judgment seems less apparent when we discover an integral connection between the aesthetic and moral realms of activity. We tend to identify activities of one type as moral and those of another type as aesthetic, perhaps partly because we believe the two to be separate, but mainly because it is simpler and more convenient to do so. However, if we admit that art has the power to enlarge and deepen the range of aesthetic sensitivity and that the aim of good art education programs is to activate that power, we can show that the sensitivity so developed has considerable bearing on moral behavior.

Since a considerable range of moral behavior is contingent on the individual's ability to show in his actions that he has some concern for his fellows, the place of sensitivity and humane feelings bears directly on morality. The faith of the Enlightenment—that through reason rather than superstition, dogma, and obedience to authority figures civilization would be increasingly humanized and enhanced —has not been borne out in practice. It is possible to contend, however, that reason has not yet been tried on a sufficiently wide scale and therefore that the Enlightenment vision may still be fulfilled. To be sure, man has used reason to improve human conditions as well as to destroy them, but unfortunately he has established far too many technological inventions and social systems only to enslave others. History is witness to the elaborate arguments used to justify slavery and to sanction inequalities and dictatorships.

As we have seen from our previous discussion, the aesthetic dimension, if properly cultivated, can enter into all areas of schooling and the larger life of man. If reason is coupled with aesthetic sensibilities, morality itself can be enhanced. Not only does man need to think reflectively about his actions and responsibilities; he needs to suffuse his actions with a sensitivity to human feelings. Each person must to some extent act on self-interest in order to protect himself and survive in the world. Usually, in fact, there is no shortage of this trait, but self-interest need not threaten the rights of others so long as a reasonable amount of human sensitivity exists. *Callousness is the antithesis of morality.* Of all traits we dare hope that man can overcome, callousness must head the list. The cultivation of aesthetic sensitivity in the manifold activities of life can nourish the roots of humaneness and usher in a greater feeling of humanity.

ART AND SOCIETY

Art may be used to advance society or to retard it. It can be employed in the promotion of human rights or of totalitarian ideals. Fortunately, many of the great figures in the arts refused to become pawns of dictators or vested interest groups. Great artists have usually proved themselves to be individualistic and independent spirits, loath to compromise their ideals.

Since artists are concerned with the expression of values, we can speak of them as constituting a community in search of values. The social nature of art arises from its basic function of expressing values, for in performing that function the artist can help society to preserve and immortalize some of its greatest achievements and historical accomplishments. Every society wants its future generations to be imbued with respect and appreciation for the principles, ideals, and deeds on which the society was founded. Art helps to memorialize the highest achievements of society in order that they may be a continuing source of inspiration for generations to come.

Art also provides aesthetic enjoyment and appreciation that are desirable for their own sakes. Art can be a source of pleasure and delight, a regenerative force in the lives of people. It has the power to add new dimensions to human lives.

Art makes a vital contribution to society by affording greater insight into the strivings of men and societies. It has the power to penetrate the masks of cant and hypocrisy by stripping away the illusions that man has created in the names of justice, honor, patriotism, and freedom. In a society that incites war fever by inducing citizens to identify with a specious patriotic mission—usually rationalized as "democracy," "freedom," or "self-determination"—the artist can counter the glorification of war by showing the brutality, suffering, and human degradation it brings in its wake. (Picasso did this in his paintings, Hemingway in his novels.) Much of the subject matter of art is contributed by the conditions of society, and the imaginative artist has usually been able to depict the real nature of these conditions in visual, literary, and musical forms. He has sometimes been able to project a vision of the consequences of existing social conditions. In other words, the artist can be the conscience of a society whose own conscience has withered, can provide a heightened sense of vision and insight into the human condition. In today's world the pace of life is so frenetic that people are averse to reflecting on where everyone is going and what the purpose of it all is. The artist can provide vision and insight into these neglected problems.

Finally, art can widen and deepen the range of human sensibilities and can cultivate the diverse modes of expression. As sensibilities are deepened and refined and the range of expression is extended, human relations may become increasingly humanized and enhanced. Thus, art at its best has the power to bring about transformations in human life by heightening man's sensitivity to his fellows.

FOR FURTHER READING

Arnstine, Donald. *Philosophy of Education: Learning and Schooling.* New York: Harper and Row, 1967.

Art Education. National Society for the Study of Education. 64th Yearbook, Part II. Chicago: University of Chicago Press, 1965.

Art in American Life and Education. National Society for the Study of Education. 40th Yearbook. Bloomington, Ill.: Public School Publishing Company, 1941.

Beardsley, Monroe C. *Aesthetics.* New York: Harcourt, Brace and World, 1958.

Bronowski, J. *Science and Human Values.* New York: Harper and Brothers, 1956.

Broudy, Harry S. "The Structure of Knowledge in the Arts," in *Education and the Structure of Knowledge.* Chicago: Rand McNally, 1964, pp. 75–119.

Cornelius, David K. and Edwin St. Vincent (eds.). *Cultures in Conflict: Perspectives on the Snow-Leavis Controversy.* Chicago: Scott, Foresman, 1964.

Dewey, John. *Art as Experience.* New York: Minton, Balch, 1935.

Ducasse, Curt John. *The Philosophy of Art.* New York: Dover Publications, 1966.

Eisner, Elliot W. and David W. Ecker. *Readings in Art Education.* Waltham, Mass.: Blaisdell, 1967.

Gotshalk, D. W. *Art and the Social Order.* Chicago: University of Chicago Press, 1947.

Hamilton, Edith. *The Great Age of Greek Literature.* New York: W. W. Norton, 1942.

Hook, Sidney (ed.). *Art and Philosophy.* New York: New York University Press, 1966.

Lowenfeld, Viktor. *Creative and Mental Growth.* New York: Macmillan, 1952.

Parker, DeWitt H. *The Principles of Aesthetics,* Second edition. New York: F. S. Crofts, 1946.

Pepper, Stephen C. *The Basis of Criticism in the Arts*. Cambridge: Harvard University Press, 1945.

Rader, Melvin (ed.). *A Modern Book of Esthetics*, Third edition. New York: Holt, Rinehart and Winston, 1960.

Read, Herbert. *Education Through Art*. London: Faber and Faber, 1943.

Rugg, Harold. *Imagination*. New York: Harper and Row, 1963.

Smith, Ralph A. (ed.). *Aesthetics and Criticism in Art Education* Chicago: Rand McNally, 1966.

The Visual Arts in General Education. Commission on Secondary School Curriculum, Progressive Education Association. New York: D. Appleton-Century, 1939.

EPILOGUE

As we look back over the intellectual terrain that we have trav-
ersed, it may be fitting at this time to examine one question alluded
to in various ways but not stated explicitly. Like others before us,
we may be unable to answer the question to our full satisfaction;
yet we now know better why it is worth raising, why it may even
deserve precedence over other questions that weigh heavily upon
us. We ask ourselves, "What does it mean to be human?"

This question is hardly new. It has been raised before in different
forms and for different reasons in the lexicons of divers philosophical systems. And answers have been provided by orthodox
and liberal theologies, political ideologies, philosophies, and psychological and psychoanalytic theories.

Of course, we cannot consider here all the solutions which have
been proffered; instead, we will follow a theme suggested earlier
in our peripatetic survey of education and human values.

Being human means having many disparate, and sometimes conflicting, attributes. In accordance with our theme, to be human is
not only to be self-conscious and aware of oneself in the world,
but to value. For man is a creature who values. If one is to be
distinctively human rather than just a vegetable devoid of striving,
searching, and choosing, he must be aware of himself in the world

and make choices that shape his future. These choices are made by reflectively assessing the situations one confronts in life. In an age which has increasingly lost faith in the ability of reason to build a future in which our highest dreams and aspirations can be fulfilled, we hear frequently that choice is irrational and baseless. Whether or not this is true, our best hope still lies in using reason to take us as far as it possibly can. The other forces will take over soon enough, for men today are pressed on all sides to yield to the blandishments of various groups—and many have indeed yielded. Even though the problems of man's existence transcend logical categories, one need not infer that a leap into irrationality is called for. To do so would be to negate the world that reason has constructed. If existing reflective tools are no longer adequate, then new ones will have to be developed. In pursuit of power and dominion over others, man has focused much of his energy on destructiveness and has built awesome weapons. Should he yearn as earnestly to bring order into the world through the resolution of social and political problems, he will create the reflective tools necessary for the task.

But man does not just value and strive to make decisions. He also yearns for some great value perspective which will unify and give meaning to his struggle. Some seek such perspective in religion, others in a political ideology. And still others elevate family group, social class, or country to a locus of values. All too frequently such maneuvers lead to accepting solutions formulated by others and to dropping out of the pursuit of direction for one's life. Man relinquishes responsibility in the hope of gaining inner peace and certainty in a world where absolute certainty is little more than a chimerical dream.

All men, irrespective of the road they choose to travel or the system of truths with which they identify, strive for the Good Life. But the Good Life has been envisioned in many ways and it is highly doubtful that men will ever reach unanimity in their depiction of it; moreover, one may indeed wonder whether such unanimity would be desirable.

What is important, however, is that to be human, to value, to strive for the Good Life, each human being must define the Good Life for himself. Perhaps this is where education comes in; it can tell us what the Good Life is or what the great minds of the past thought it was. Education can provide us with a broad cultural understanding as well as sharpen our abilities of reflective thinking. Most of all, it can give us the desire for lifetime education and provide a basis for continuing self-education. Unfortunately for many of today's youth, education does not succeed in attaining these goals. But even the person fortunate enough to have had an education that did so must assume individual responsibility for working out what he believes the Good Life ultimately to be. Those who are conscious of their existence and capable of making independent value judgments realize that life is short and fleeting and that it should not go for naught. They impel themselves forward, formulating and reconstructing their conception of the Good Life as they strive each day to make more intelligent value decisions.

The road is strewn with many obstacles, as we have seen in the preceding chapters. Each person is born into a culture permeated with values, many of them conflicting, and he dies in a culture—usually though not always the same one. Each person, therefore, is born, lives, and dies within a cultural matrix of competing values. The attitudes he takes and the decisions he makes in reference to these values will determine the quality of his life. Any person who aspires to live his life on an especially high level will probably have to have values higher than those of his culture. He may set an example for others to follow, but he should not expect to be understood. However, this in no way means that such a person will habitually violate the laws of his society, although he may occasionally disobey a specific law that runs counter to his moral principles. He will not hide this fact by performing his action clandestinely; he is more likely to act publicly and to assume full responsibility for his actions.

We have assumed throughout that the individual lives in a relatively open society that provides a modicum of freedom of choice. In such a society he can be proud of and grateful for the rights and opportunities provided; yet in all societies there are cultural patterns and tendencies that are inimical to the full and healthy growth of persons. Each individual needs to make a rational assessment of the conditions that promote such growth and those that injure, distort, and hamper human development and slow down the humanization of man's relation to man. The individual alone must decide what role he will play in his culture's future. But he would be hard-pressed if he tried to justify a choice of complete withdrawal.

Born into a culture and having a relatively short span of life, man seeks to relate himself productively to his world. Our technological advances and the resulting complexities of organizational structure have not been an unmixed blessing, for man has experienced a loss of satisfaction and meaning in work and a diminution of his productive orientation. Certainly not all material advances can be called "progress" in view of the destructive and dehumanizing forces that they sometimes unleash. Yet we cannot turn the clock back to some bygone age of imaginary pristine purity; those who daydream about some golden age in the past often overlook the wretched conditions that actually existed at the time. Nor can we sacrifice the present for an unknowable future by violently over-throwing existing institutions in the hope of ushering in a utopian state. For invariably a greater tyranny replaces the one overthrown. Furthermore, we do not find acceptable utopian habits of mind which would separate means from ends and commit atrocities in the present for the sake of an illusory dream in the future. Man is confronted with the obdurate fact that he must work within the present and deal with people and institutions of his own time. He will have to find ways of maintaining present advances and of encouraging their future growth; yet he will also have to find the means to recognize the system so that he may once again enjoy a productive orientation toward work and toward life.

Man cannot be fully human unless he invariably makes inde-pendent moral judgments, assumes full responsibility for them, and strives to construct a meaningful system of values. Those without serious psychological deficiencies, who have filled their cups with a sufficient amount of respect, recognition, security, and affection and have drunk heartily of the heady wine, have created self-actualizing tendencies to support moral autonomy. There is a more arduous path. It involves questioning the most fundamental values of one's culture, those that one has lived by; it means courageously facing the abyss of nihilism that Nietzsche knew so well. At that point one is in a position to reconstruct his value system.

To be fully human is to be fully conscious, to experience the great sorrows and joys of life. Those not fully conscious live in a gray world of depression, never aware of the heights and depths of the human spirit. Aesthetic sensitivity enables one to appreciate life in its multiple and variegated dimensions. To know tragedy, one must first have tasted the joy and exhilaration of life. Through aesthetic sensitivity one is able to perceive moral choices in a wider and deeper dimension.

There are many who choose not to be fully human, lose their individuality by accepting values ready-made from a source outside themselves, from some ideological dogma that promises certainty in return for unquestioning loyalty. But those who choose the lifelong quest for the answer to the question, "What does it mean to be human?" will be buoyed in their adventure by their efforts to become fully conscious, aesthetically sensitive, and morally autonomous as they seek their own construction of the Good Life.

INDEX

Hospers, John, 98
Humanistic psychology, 30
Huxley, Aldous, 130

Industrial Revolution, 130
International community, 19–21

Jones, Vernon, 114, 123
Jourard, Sidney M., 118, 123

Kaufmann, Walter, 123
Kimball, Solon T., 35
Kneller, George F., 80
Kohlberg, Lawrence, 120, 123
Kohn, Hans, 17
Komisar, B. Paul, 31
Krathwohl, David R., 134

Learning, domains of, 134–135
Lieberman, Myron, 73
Lindeman, Eduard C., 26
Lowenfeld, Viktor, 153

McClellan, James E., Jr., 35
McClelland, David C., 35
March, James G., 65, 76
Marx, Karl, 18
Masia, Bertram B., 134
Maslow, Abraham H., 30, 31,
     74, 77, 79, 89, 117, 118,
     123, 138, 139
Mausner, Bernard, 75, 76
May, M. A., 112, 120, 123
Mayo, Elton, 44
Medlin, Brian, 92
Melden, A. I., 97
Merton, Robert K., 77
Michael, Donald N., 35
Mill, John Stuart, 4
Mills, C. Wright, 39
Money-Kyrle, R. E., 117
Monney, James D., 41
Moral autonomy, 78–83
Moral development
     character traits, 112–113
     habit, 113–114
     rules, 111
Moral judgments
     data, use of, 102–103
     hierarchy of values, 103–104

intentions, 98–100
principles, 106
process of, 100
validation, 109
way of life, 107–108, 110
Moral life
     natural state, 96–97
     religious justifications, 93–96
     self-interest, 91–93
Morality
     authority, 86
     commitment, 89–90
     conscience, 84–86
     punishment, fear of, 87–88
Moral values and art; see
     Aesthetic sensitivity
Mortimer, R. C., 94, 96
Moustakas, Clark E., 123

Nagel, Ernest, 3
Neurosis, 116–117
Newman, Fred W., 13
Niblett, W. R., 89, 113
Niebuhr, Reinhold, 19
Nietzsche, Friedrich, 18, 89,
     99, 158
Nowell-Smith, P. H., 85, 94,
     123

Oliver, Donald W., 13
Organizational authority, 54–55
     charisma, 54
     delegation of, 47
     types of, 55
Organizational control
     rules, 54
     standards, 54
Organizational disorder, 53
Organizational goals
     displacement, 46
     educational, 46, 49
     general, 45
     and philosophy of education,
     49
     specific, 45
Organizations
     groups, informal, 42–44, 47
     ideal type, 39
     innovation, resistance to, 64